Blessed Assurance

Tim Georgeff

Published by Tim Georgeff, 2024.

BLESSED ASSURANCE

First edition. March 5, 2024.

ISBN: 979-8223743279

Written by Tim Georgeff.

For every single person who prayed, for all those who supported and cared for us, and for anyone seeking faith and hope in their lives, this is for you.

For my wife, Shelley, I would do it all over again. You are my sky full of stars.

The Post

Hey friends, we need
some serious prayer.
Shelley had a brain
aneurysm last night and
is having emergency
surgery right now.

. . . .

TYPING AND POSTING that to Facebook was one of the toughest decisions of my life. I needed help. I needed an outlet, some way of getting this panic out of me. Additionally, I felt guilty, like I was betraying my wife's privacy. I also wasn't being completely honest. My wife had suffered one of the worst aneurysms a person could have, a hemorrhage of her carotid artery, and the doctors had prepared me to accept the reality she was not going to make it. These twenty-one words did not accurately represent how dire the circumstances were, or my actual emotional state. I was pretending to be brave, the stoic family leader, but in reality, I was a complete mess. I never could have known the kind of miracles one seemingly innocent, yet desperate post would initiate. At the time I started writing this book, close to three million people had viewed the video of my wife taking her first steps after waking up from her coma. There are tens of thousands of prayers written on social media as well as sent by email and text. Maybe you read my updates, maybe someone you know shared the story with you, or maybe you are curious to know the story behind the posts. Maybe you need to be reassured that miracles can and do happen, or maybe you need a miracle yourself. This book is for all of you.

I lost my mom when I was thirty-four years old. She was way too young to die, and I was way too young to accept it. Diagnosed with stage four brain and lung cancer, she lived three agonizing months before slipping into a coma and dying. It happened during a three-year period where I lost my mom, both her parents (my grandparents), and my dad's brother. If there was ever a time in my life I needed a miracle, it was then. I learned during that time that everyone suffers loss. While we go on remembering those we have lost for a long period of time, others move on from suffering through that loss with us, to consoling others who are experiencing loss, or dealing with loss of their own. Just reading that back to myself makes my head spin, but I think where I want that point to land is this: there comes a time where we find ourselves alone in our grief. My wife, Shelley, rescued me from that dark place.

So, when she found herself battling for her life, I desired nothing more than to save her, to be her hero, to repay her for rescuing me. But instead, I found myself powerless, unable to truly do anything effectively myself, desperately needing a miracle. So, I started praying. Actually, if I want to be honest about it, I asked someone else to pray first. Then I asked everyone else to pray before I really laid into it. I also began to write. Writing was both a way to keep everyone up to date as well as for my own therapeutic release. I never expected the overwhelming response I received to my daily updates. Even right this second, it seems ridiculous to me that I am writing a book about this experience, except people keep asking me to do it. They read all the posts, and they want to know more about what happened, but that isn't enough to write a book. God gave us a miracle, and if we are to be obedient to His calling for us, then we need to share the testimony we were given.

I would ask why, but I am curious myself. I know I am a radically different person after going through this experience, but how I got here and what changed is only going to be deciphered by my own self exploration. I think the only way for me to remind myself, for me to teach others, and maybe render aid to someone else is to put the words on paper for anyone who is interested in reading them. Although I have spent many years leading worship in a church, I am no Theologian. Although I may throw a verse or two out at you, this is not meant to be a Bible study. This isn't a feel-good book or screenplay about someone who died, saw Jesus, and came back to tell us about it. This is the gritty truth about how my anger at God changed my perspective on prayer and obedience, and it is a description of the trial my wife and I experienced, the suffering and refinement we both endured, and the drastic effect it had on our lives. Looking back, it also explores the humor of certain situations, the prayers, the responses, and the way we were able to survive the roller coaster of emotions.

Maybe readers will find ways to handle their grief, deal with trials of their own, or cradle a nugget of hope that manifests itself into a miracle for them or someone they love. Just understand, as we uncover and pull back the curtain on what happened, you may rethink the way you love, your future expectations, and most assuredly, the responsibility that comes with prayer. I can think of no other way to say it than this: Be careful what you pray for.

Tuesday, April 4th – The Incident

It was one of those perfect nights. We had just finished our regular Tuesday night gig at Chamberlain's Steak and Chop House. The piano lounge there is a lot of fun, and we had built up a good following for an early weeknight. We had even met a nice couple that wanted to book us for a private event toward the end of the year. We walked out that night with our tip jar full, a private event ready to go to contract, and enjoying our ride home together singing new songs, laughing, and talking about what we had planned for the rest of the week.

We arrived home just before midnight. It was quite breezy, a couple late spring pop-up thunderstorms had blown through, and I decided to check the gates and chicken coops to make sure all the animals were safely tucked away. It was eerie out in the dark, and I was using the light on my phone to make sure I didn't walk through a spiderweb or trip on a random tool or farm implement in the dark. We had over sixty eggs in three incubators in our kitchen, and the first batch was ready to hatch at any moment, so I wasn't surprised to see my phone screen light up with Shelley's number.

"Come inside, quick," she spit out rapidly.

"I'll be right in, I am almost done," I replied. I suspected the chickens were hatching, and she wanted me to see them.

"Come inside, now." The phone went dead. Strange. I reversed course and headed for the kitchen door. The little dogs were still outside in the backyard, and the big dogs were waiting by the kitchen door, expecting some food or to be put to bed. I entered the house; Shelley was not in the kitchen and a quick look in the incubators showed no signs of new life.

"Where are you babe?"

No answer. The house was still mostly dark other than the kitchen light. I made my way through the living room and turned down the short hallway into our bedroom. Dim light spilled from the master closet through the master bathroom and onto the bed. Shelley was sitting on the side of it holding her head.

"What's wrong," I asked. She had not complained about a headache all day. Shelley had frequent headaches that bordered on migraines; and had suffered from them for over twenty-five years. Doctors could never really pinpoint what the cause was, and she had learned to live with them the best she could.

"My head feels like it is going to explode. I need help."

"Do you want some Advil or Tylenol?"

"No, I need you to call 9-1-1. I think I am about to die."

Two things you need to know about my wife Shelley. One, when she says call an ambulance, you don't ask why. Two, she rarely exaggerates when it comes to her health. I once saw her break her back and she calmly told me not to move her and call an ambulance. I have watched her carry her toenail in the palm of her hand while limping in from the pasture, lie down on the floor of the dining room, and ask me to get a band-aid for her toe that required stitches to fix and a fake toenail for over a year. I have also seen her butterfly bandage a cut on her own forehead because the scar would be in her eyebrow, and it was a waste of time to have the doctor do it. So, when she said call an ambulance, I didn't question the moment at all. The operator told me Whitewright Emergency Services was responding and were about ten to fifteen minutes out. If there is any drawback to living in the country, it is at a moment like this. Waiting is excruciating.

I asked Shelley what I could do to help her, but she just shook her head, holding it in her hands while rocking back and forth on the side of the bed. I hurried out to the end of the driveway, manually opened the automatic gates, put the big dogs up in the garage and brought the little dogs inside. When I reentered the bedroom, Shelley was still holding her head and rocking.

"Call them again. Tell them I need help now."

I dialed 9-1-1 again and tried to impress upon the operator that we needed help now. She assured me that the nearest emergency team was responding and less than ten minutes out.

"I am going to throw up," Shelley said.

I grabbed the wastebasket from the bathroom, dumped the trash on the floor, and put it next to the bed. Not a moment too soon, as Shelley leaned over and began throwing up into it. For a few minutes I sat there near her feet with my hand on her leg, not wanting to disturb her, unsure of the severity of what was happening. I couldn't tell if this was a severe migraine or something else entirely. I cursed under my breath quietly, straining to hear an approaching ambulance. I got up with the intention of going to the front door to see if they were arriving, but Shelley stopped me.

"I don't want to die alone."

The words were barely a whisper, yet they sucked all the air out of the room, my ears started ringing and I knew something was really wrong. The dogs started barking like crazy. The ambulance must have come sirens off because of the late hour.

"I'll be right back, honey, I have to let them in." I sprinted out the door and around the front of the house to the ambulance. The two young men were already grabbing their things, and I relayed to them what was happening inside. The next ten minutes were a blur of questions, checking vitals, and Shelley's insistence they get her to the hospital immediately. They finally got her loaded up in the ambulance, started an IV, and then asked me if I was going to ride or follow.

"I am going to follow," I said, thinking about the over 100 animals we had on our farm. Shelley was trying to argue somewhat incoherently that she wanted me to ride in the ambulance, but I wasn't sure how long we would be in the Emergency Room. I probably needed to be prepared to come home and let the dogs out in the morning. I assured her it would be okay and exited the back of the ambulance and got into my car. The ambulance turned on its lights and pulled out of the driveway, me following right behind, and we headed toward Texoma Medical Center in Denison, Texas.

Wednesday, April 5th – The Diagnosis

Texoma Medical Center is a good-sized regional hospital located between Sherman and Denison in far North Texas. Even though it is always moderately busy, I was able to find a parking place very close to the Emergency entrance and was with Shelley as they pulled her out of the back of the ambulance and took her inside.

The next two hours consisted of visits by several nurses and doctors, the administering of migraine medication, and a lot of waiting. Shelley continued to alternate between sitting up with her head between her knees, rocking back and forth holding her head, and lying back nearly unconscious. When it appeared that no amount of medication was going to help her, they decided to start running scans on her. She was gone for about 30 minutes, and when they brought her back, a doctor was with her and immediately began pouring out a flood of information onto me. It was such a jumble of medical terms and test results I couldn't take it all in, but I remember hearing words and short phrases including hemorrhaging, bleeding, cranial pressure, extremely sick, most likely not going to make it...

I stopped the doctor right there. What? Shelley was still semi-conscious, holding her head and moaning, and I asked the doctor to step out of the room. I asked him to slow down and start over. He began again, explaining that Shelley had an enormous amount of blood in her cranial cavity, that there was an aneurysm or hemorrhage in or near her carotid artery, but it was hard to fully diagnose and see because of all the blood and trauma inside her brain. I asked him how it could be treated and what the next step would be, and he explained to me that he most likely needed to reduce the pressure from the bleed by cutting into or draining her cranial cavity, and he felt confident he could do that, but beyond providing some temporary relief from the pain, they were not equipped to save my wife's life in this hospital. She was lucky to have lived long enough to make it to the hospital, but there was not much hope for her.

It seemed like the lights in the hallway dimmed. I felt blackness rushing in on me from all sides. There was a humming in my ears, and I felt my heart stop beating.

"You can't save her?"

"Sir, your wife is extremely sick," the doctor said slowly. "There is a lot of blood in and around her brain. We do not have the required technology or personnel here to save her life. I'm sorry, have you notified the rest of your family?"

I slumped against the wall, my wife less than twenty feet from my back, and for a moment was paralyzed from the words the doctor had just said.

"Her family lives all over the country," I said, the words sounding dumb even as they were coming out of my mouth. "You think I should call them and have them come here?"

"Like I said, she is extremely sick and was lucky to even make it to the hospital. I think you should call them and inform them what is happening."

I blinked back the tears in my eyes. If I were to try and describe what this moment felt like, everything in the world around me had gone into extreme slow motion. I could see nurses and staff staring at me, nobody was moving, I couldn't hear anything, even the doctor in front of me was frozen. Meanwhile in my head, there was a rush of memories and visions flashing by rapidly, like fast-forward on a television. I don't know how long this sensation lasted, but it felt like an eternity, and then suddenly there was a convergence, the real world and my memories crashing together with a thunderous boom, an explosion of light, and everything was back moving at a normal pace. Beeps and whistles from medical devices, the droning sound of medical personnel talking in rooms and hallways through the hospital, the moaning of my wife rocking back and forth holding her head, it was a symphony of sound I would come to dread in the coming weeks.

"Somebody help me," she cried out.

I looked at the doctor who was still standing in front of me, arms at his sides, looking for all intents and purposes like he was defeated.

"Is there anything else we can do?"

"We are asking some of the hospitals in Dallas if they have a bed available. They are much better equipped for a situation like this. But I must tell you, it is highly unlikely that she will make it there," the doctor said.

"But there is something they can do? It is possible they can help her?"

"Sir, from what I can see on your wife's scans, the carotid artery is leaking an enormous amount of blood into your wife's skull. How severe the damage is, I cannot tell. It is hard to see on the scans, but she may have had a slow bleed or leak, probably an aneurysm, for a while before it burst. The bleeding from an injury like this usually leads to death within a matter of minutes. Most patients never even make it to a hospital. There are specialty units at larger hospitals that are better equipped to deal with trauma like this. That is the next logical step. We are doing our best to find a place to take her. I will be back as soon as we have found a place and transportation for her. Most likely we will be using air transport to Parkland Hospital in Dallas. We will begin preparing her for that shortly."

The next forty-five minutes was another blur of activity. Nurses were checking Shelley's vitals continuously while preparing us for air transport. At one point they took us out onto the tarmac, the helicopter and pilots ready to take us to Dallas. We waited as thunderstorms rumbled all around us and the wind gusted and swirled. Finally, they informed us we would not be able to go, the weather was too dangerous. We went back into the ER, back to the room we had recently left. Shelley was mostly unconscious, and for a moment I felt all alone. Completely and utterly without any idea of what to do, I was freezing up mentally, not sure what the next step was, or how I could help my wife.

I sighed and looked at my phone, I didn't have all of Shelley's family programmed into it. I pulled Shelley's phone out of my back pocket. I needed to figure out quickly what to say, and how to prevent as much panic as possible. It would be easiest to send this from her phone, she already had a group chat with most of her family on it. I don't know why, but I decided to text her youngest daughter separately on my phone first, and to do so with as little information as possible. She lived closest to us, about three and a half hours away in Tulsa, and I didn't want her to make the decision to drive down without speaking to me first. I had the feeling I was not going to be getting home to let the dogs out or feed any animals – something Logann was well versed at doing.

Wed, Apr 5 at 4:19 AM - Logann, I need you to text me the minute you wake up, it's an emergency. Do not call, text me, please. Or if you can get down here, please do so safely.

I hit send on my phone. Shelley was moaning in pain again, her hands covering her face. It was 4:23am, and I dreaded making phone calls to family in the middle of the night. What would I even say? I opened Facebook Messenger to see if the little green dots were on next to any familiar names. Maybe some of her family or our friends had insomnia and I could call someone, anyone...

A little green dot was next to the first face in the top left corner of the screen. Our pastor, Jason. What were the chances of that?

Brother, I need a prayer. Shelley had a brain hemorrhage and it's not looking good. We are at Texoma Medical waiting for air transport to any hospital in Dallas that can do a surgery immediately. It's life threatening. I don't want to blast it publicly or anything, I need to notify all her family first, but I need help.

Praying right now Brother... I'm currently in west Texas (hauling) or I'd be right there...Sorry I can't be with you.

It's all in God's hands. I know you would be here if you could. I just need my strongest prayer warrior on this, and you are that man.

Our pastor, Jason Norton, is the type of man you want looking out for you in any crisis, physical or spiritual. A former Army Ranger and SWAT team member, Jason taught from the pulpit out of the Bible in a humble yet commanding manner. His knowledge of The Word was exceptional, and his conviction was unwavering. Just knowing he was aware and praying for my wife helped steady me. I was also confident he would know what prayer to pray. That may sound strange, but I felt like the right prayer was crucial at this moment.

I went to my wife's side and rubbed her arm while looking at her. No visible change. Her hands still covered her face, but she was not responsive to my voice or touch. A nurse peeked in, asked if we wanted the light off, and I mumbled some sort of affirmative response. I put my phone down and picked up Shelley's. I stared at it not knowing what to type. The doctor appeared at the door and beckoned me out into the hallway.

"Sir, we are going to take her in a bus to Medical City Plano. They have a unit there that specializes in this type of medical emergency. If she can make it there alive, there may be options for them there we are not able to do here."

"A bus?"

"An ambulance, lights on, we need to go now. I think it is best if you drive your own car there. It is going to be crowded in the back of the bus and they are going to be going extremely fast."

"Okay. Medical City Plano, you said?"

"Yes, we are going now."

Shelley's bed was already being whisked by me, and I chased it out the doors. They stopped at the back of the ambulance. She was unconscious, so I just kissed her forehead and squeezed her hand. As they loaded her up, I sent a text to the rest of Shelley's family.

Wed, Apr 5 at 4:38 AM - This is Tim on Shelley's phone. She had a cerebral hemorrhage last night and the situation is life threatening. We are awaiting transport from the regional hospital in Sherman to Medical City Plano. The doctor says she has had a slow bleed in her carotid artery that has filled up the area around her brain. They need to do emergency surgery to try and relieve that ASAP. She is barely conscious, and I am unable to take any calls about this right now. I will update everyone as soon as we get her moved and into surgery. This is all the info I have at this time, and I don't want to cause a panic, but the doctor felt it would be best to notify all our family. I don't think there is anything anyone can do at this point, it's in the doctor's and God's hands.

That text went to Shelley's sisters, mom, dad, and eldest daughter. All lived quite a distance from us and would require travel plans to get to Dallas. The ambulance was getting ready to leave, and I hopped in my car to follow, unsure of what would happen next. My phone beeped an alert for an incoming text. It was Shelley's sister, Keri.

Tracy is on her way. Mom and I are finding flights. Do I need to call Rach and Lo?

I texted them, no reply yet. Keri, I want to warn you it's not looking good. She's not conscious right now. They are preparing to move her right now.

Ok Tim. We are coming. I will take care of the girls Is she breathing on her own, or no?

The ambulance was pulling away, and I called Keri so I could drive and talk. I don't remember a thing we spoke about; I was having a hard time following the ambulance through the tears filling my eyes. The best I can recall, Keri filled me in on the travel plans and that she would take care of talking with the family so I could focus on getting to the hospital with Shelley.

I never lost track of the lights of the ambulance, but they did manage to get a pretty large lead on me right away. "Lights on" meant they were blowing through every stop light and stop sign, and I still needed to heed traffic laws. Once we were on the highway from Sherman to Plano, I realized I would have had to exceed the speed limit by an amount I wasn't comfortable with to catch back up, and I also felt the need to call my father. So, I kept the blinking lights in sight up ahead and dialed up my dad. It was just a little past 5:30AM CST, and he was home in Michigan where it was just past 6:30AM. He probably would figure something was out of the ordinary for me to be calling this early.

I explained to him what was going on, and he was ready to fly down with his wife, Carol, right away; however, I told him to slow down and wait at least for a few hours while I figured out what was happening. I was in tears when I told him I wasn't sure if he should be packing to help at the hospital or packing a suit for a funeral. I could tell he was really torn up by this situation, the experience we went through when we lost my mother had left deep scars. Later, once things were a little clearer, he would tell me he never had any doubts. In fact, he told me that God had reassured him on the drive down to Texas, giving him the overwhelming feeling everything would be okay. For now, though, he was feeling the mental anguish I was experiencing.

I hung up and saw a notification on my Facebook messenger from Pastor Jason.

I called Molly and prayed together... We're still praying... We love yawl and tell Shelley we're praying for her...

Thank you. They are moving her to Medical City Plano now.
Hallelujah!

Jason was already praising the Lord. I wished I had the confidence our pastor had at that moment. I drove the rest of the way in silence, asking God over and over in my head why this was happening. We had been through so much in the past three years, and it just didn't seem fair for this to be happening when we had finally found ourselves in a good rhythm, working as much as we wanted, leading music at our church and several others, and enjoying time with family and friends in a home where we could see ourselves retiring. We had forty-six acres of beautiful pastures with over a dozen rescue horses, longhorn cattle, goats, chickens, pigs, and even kangaroos. Rounding out our personal zoo were several dogs and cats, and two beautiful little puppies that were due to go to their new homes this week. In fact, one owner had flown in from California expecting to meet us today... Crap!

I found a parking spot near the ER doors and scrolled through Shelley's phone. I found the texts she had been exchanging with the owner of the puppy. I saw they were supposed to meet at 12:30 PM today.

Wed, Apr 5 at 6:26 AM - Reagan, this is Shelley's husband Tim. Sorry to text you so early – Shelley suffered a cerebral hemorrhage late last night and we are awaiting emergency surgery right now. I know you are flying out today and am trying to figure out a way to get you your puppy. I will not be able to meet at the house at 12:30, but I'm hoping I can have someone pick the puppy up and bring her down toward Dallas so we can get her to you. Please bear with me as I figure out the logistics of all this, and I will call later this morning once I have figured out a plan.

I figured she probably would think we were trying to scam her out of her deposit money after reading that text, but I really didn't have time to worry about it anymore. I was assuming we were going to be having surgery as soon as they took her in. I scanned through my phone and saw a little chatter from family members saying they were on their way. I looked up at the ambulance parked under the porte-cochere. Shelley had already been wheeled through the double sliding glass doors directly into the emergency room area. I ran to those doors, but the security officer waved me toward the public doors a couple hundred feet away. I pointed at Shelley's head, still visible at the top of the bed as paramedics were pushing her into a room right around the corner and yelled to him that she was my wife. He shook his head and pointed again. I screamed at him to open the doors and one of the paramedics saw me and came back and let me through. The guard stepped forward, but paused when he saw my face, and probably recognized the look in my eyes. I hate to think how many times he has looked into the eyes of someone losing a family member.

Inside the room, Shelley was moaning on the bed, hands over her face. Several nurses were attempting to get vitals and a triage specialist was yelling at Shelley, asking her name, if she knew where she was; trying to get any response, of which there was none. I did my best to describe what had happened at our house, and what I had observed and been told at the other hospital. The doctor and nurses left armed with all the information they could collect after telling me they would be sending Shelley for imaging.

The door closed and for a moment it was quiet. I knelt on the floor next to the bed and grabbed one of Shelley's hands. There was no resistance as I pulled it away from her face, her eyes were closed, but her face was scrunched up in pain, and she made groaning noises as she tried to breathe. I told her I loved her and explained where we were and what was going on. There was no response.

The door burst open and suddenly she was gone, whisked away to imaging. I thought they mentioned a CT scan, but I had now been awake for over twenty-four hours straight, and was not doing well with understanding anything going on at the moment. I sat alone in the small room, hearing the bustle of a busy morning shift. I would also later learn we arrived at one of the worst times. Shift change is at 7:00AM, and by arriving slightly before that, we were coming in at the end of a shift and the nurses and doctors that did the initial assessment were responsible for handing off all their patients to the incoming shift.

As quickly as she was gone, she was back. She was on a different bed; this one had a monitor and several bags of fluid attached to it. Shelley had a new IV stuck in her, and the monitor had several cables running to her on different parts of her body. The nurses parked her bed and said someone would be in with the results of the testing shortly.

The monitor was making quite a racket with several alarms going off, and a nurse had to keep coming in to check on Shelley and reset the monitor. I could tell the noise was really disturbing her. Finally, the nurse got the monitor muted and left us alone in the room.

"Honey, can you hear me," I asked, hoping for some sort of response.

Nothing.

We waited for about thirty minutes. After what seemed an eternity, several doctors and nurses all came in at once. They began explaining to me a scenario very similar to what I had heard up at Texoma Medical. One of the doctors introduced herself as one of the leaders of the stroke team in the ER. She mentioned that due to all the pressure and bleeding in her brain, Shelley was most likely experiencing stroke damage, and to stop that from continuing they needed to release the pressure. She continued to explain there were two ways of doing this. If Shelley passed a neurological exam, they could insert an EVD, or external ventricular drain, into her head to drain the excess blood out and maintain a safe cranial pressure. If she didn't pass a neurological exam, they would perform a craniotomy, where they would cut away a large portion of her skull to relieve the pressure. I asked what the neurological exam consisted of. The doctor told me I was about to find out, and the next five minutes were total chaos.

"Can you tell me your name," the doctor yelled at Shelley in a high-pitched voice. "Do you know where you are? Can you tell me your name?"

No response.

"Shelley, can you hear me? Tell me where you are. Can you hear me?"

Still no response.

When Shelley has bad headaches, she doesn't talk. She pulls the curtains shut, pulls a sheet over her head, and she doesn't talk to ANYONE. I knew if what she was feeling in her head was as bad or worse than one of those headaches, she surely wasn't going to answer this doctor that was shrieking these questions at her. I bent down near her head and talked to her gently.

"Babe, you need to say something to these doctors. If you don't, they are going to cut your skull open. I know you are in there; I know you can hear me, help me out here."

Shelly was still motionless.

"Honey, please, I know you don't want to, but you need to do this, PLEASE."

I looked at the doctor and she shook her head.

"Okay, we are going to take her up to surgery now for the craniotomy."

They pushed the bed out of the room and started down the hallway.

"Wait! I know she is in there and able to speak," I told the doctor. "She gets like this when she has a bad headache, and won't speak to anyone. Please, there must be some other way to check."

"God, please give her a nudge. I know she is still in there," I prayed out loud. There was something really bothering me about her undergoing a craniotomy. I did not feel confident she would make it out of that alive.

The stroke doctor looked at me, reached over to Shelley with one hand, grabbed her skin on the front of her armpit that runs between her shoulder and chest and pinched and twisted with all her might. Shelley sat straight up in the bed, her eyes open wide, and she looked straight into the doctor's face.

"Stop hurting me! That hurts!"

Shelley laid her head back down on the pillow.

"Let's go for the EVD," the doctor said.

"Wait," Shelley's voice was weak, but still loud enough for the nurses to hear.

Shelley reached out with her hand toward me. I leaned over her and took her hand.

"I love you," I said, looking directly into her eyes.

"I love you, too."

Those would be the last words we would speak to one another for quite a while.

It was still sometime on the morning of April 5th. We had moved up onto the fourth floor of the hospital in the Neuro ICU. I was able to stay in the room with her for a little while, but she was unconscious, and they finally asked me to go down to the waiting room while the Neurosurgeon that was on-call performed the surgery to put the EVD in her brain. Their first goal was to get the cranial pressure down, drain all the blood and spinal fluid that was built up in her brain, and then explore what had happened to the carotid artery and see if there was a way to fix the leak. There was so much blood in the area, scans were unable to conclusively show them what was happening. One of the doctors had a thick stack of paperwork for me to sign. While going through it, she explained to me that the aneurysm and hemorrhage Shelley was suffering from usually killed the patient before they made it to the hospital, and of those patients that made it to the ER, most never made it off the operating table. If the EVD was successful in stabilizing Shelley, we still had a long road ahead of us, and I should be planning for a long stay in the ICU. The typical hospital stay for someone in this position was twenty-one days in the ICU, followed by additional time in step down units, finally following up with extensive rehabilitation. This was all contingent on them being able to start draining all the fluid in her brain and stopping the bleeding. Once the EVD was completed and she was stabilized, they would take some more scans and the surgeons would decide what path they would want to take. It was also mentioned she may need to be ventilated to help her breathe. I watched as a handful of nurses swarmed around her, starting new IV's, adding an arterial line, and hooking up numerous wires and diodes to her body. The number of machines pumping medication into her was too much for one cart, and a second was brought in. I counted eight of these devices dripping meds into her IV lines. The doctor had me sign one final form. It was a "do not resuscitate" form, and I had to make sure I was reading and signing correctly. By signing the form, I was indicating I wanted the doctors to attempt to save her in case of an emergency, even if it left her incapacitated or handicapped. Shelley and I had jokingly talked about these things before, but I never thought I would have to make choices like this for my wife while she was 49 years old. The weight of these decisions was crushing down on me, it was a lot of information to try and take in while lacking sleep and being emotionally charged. They asked me one final question as I was walking out the door.

"Do you mind if we shave her head?"

I looked at Shelley. She was still wearing full makeup and her hair was done from our gig the night before. Looking at her, you never would have guessed the severity of the medical emergency. I considered the ramifications of what she would say if she woke up bald, so I asked if they had to shave it all. We discussed it briefly and they showed me that for now they could get away with shaving a small portion of her scalp covering the area between the top of her ear going up on top of her head behind her eye. That would have to do.

I wandered down the hall, lost in a fog of grief, lack of sleep, and overwhelmed senses. The waiting area just outside the ICU was a dark room with some alcoves and nooks, several televisions, a large saltwater fish tank, tables, chairs, and several small couches. A few people were scattered around, most looking like how I felt I must look. I did not feel like sitting, so I wandered back out, and began a slow circuit of pacing from the elevators to the waiting room, and down to Shelley's room and back. The curtains were drawn, but I could see several pairs of shoes hovering around the bed. They were doing the surgery right in the room. I stopped pacing and looked at my phone which had been silenced. I had a missed call from my dad, so I took a minute to text him an update.

Wed, Apr 5 at 8:30 AM - Waiting on surgeons to decide what they want to do. Her carotid artery has burst, and she has a lot of blood on her brain. They are talking about her being in the ICU for three weeks or more if surgery is successful. She is somewhat stabilized right now but not awake. May have to put her on a ventilator if she doesn't get more responsive soon. Her family is coming so I don't need immediate help, but I might need help if it's as long term as they say it's going to be.

I was still standing outside her room, leaning against the wall. There was nothing to see, but I couldn't force myself to go back down to the waiting room. I felt someone approaching me, surely an ICU nurse telling me to scram, but when I turned my head to look, I saw our pastor's wife, Molly. She didn't say a word, just put her arms around me and hugged me hard. Then she prayed for Shelley, for me, for the doctors, and the nurses. She put her hand right on the window of Shelley's room, praying for the machines and the medication. It was short but powerful.

I did my best to explain what was going on, and we watched and waited outside the room. It was hard to believe so much had happened in less than twelve hours. Shelley's sister, Keri, had taken care of getting the family informed and traveling to the hospital, it seemed like I had the first part of the day under control, and everything else was in God's hands.

The doctors finally exited the room, and the surgeon and one of his assistants came directly to me. They explained that the EVD had been successfully inserted into her brain. They explained that an external ventricular drain (EVD) is a catheter that is inserted via a burr hole into the anterior horn of the lateral ventricle and connected to a closed sterile system to allow for temporary drainage of cerebrospinal fluid (CSF) and/or monitoring of intracranial pressure. There was a large bag already filling with fluid that was dark red, and another number on the digital display above Shelley's head showing intercranial pressure (ICP). This would allow the pressure in her cranial cavity to be monitored and modified to attempt to keep any more damage from happening to the tissue and blood vessels in the brain. This would also allow them to get better imaging of the damaged carotid and possibly even perform an angiogram to start getting a better picture of how they might attempt to fix the damage. There would be a few minutes to see her before they began preparing to take her.

Tracy, Shelley's sister, was the first family member to arrive with her husband and son. I met them near the elevators and explained to the best of my ability what was going on. She walked with me down to Shelley's room and we both looked at her lying in the bed. The number of tubes, diodes, wires, and hoses going in and out of her body was overwhelming, but her face looked peaceful and serene. It was hard not to break down, but we managed to talk to Shelley soothingly and sit by her for a few minutes. Tracy told me she would be on the lookout for the rest of the family as they were coming into town; her other sister, Keri, from Florida, her daughter, Rachael, and mother, Darlene, from California, her father, Ron, from Nevada, and her daughter, Logann, driving in from Tulsa.

I was left alone for a few minutes, and I contemplated what I was about to do. I have never been a huge fan of using social media for anything other than business. I never much cared for reading other people's personal and family problems, and never understood why people wanted to make their personal issues so public. I was struggling with how I was going to notify people of what was going on, and I was feeling called to get some people praying. I also knew once word got out, there was going to be a massive response. There were a lot of people who kept track of Shelley Luther. In case you are not familiar with her name, she was the Dallas Salon owner who reopened her business during the Covid-19 shutdowns. When forced to appear in court and threatened with one-hundred eighty days in jail unless she apologized and shut her salon back down, she respectfully stood up to the judge and was jailed. The absurdity of what was being done to her made international news and inspired a movement for people to take back their personal liberties and rights. I needed to find a way to inform everyone and honor her privacy. I finally pulled the trigger and posted one post on Facebook.

Hey friends, we need some serious prayer. Shelley had a brain aneurysm last night and is having emergency surgery right now.

Even though I knew the news would get some attention, I was not ready for the response. My phone began vibrating from incoming messages and texts almost instantaneously. I didn't even attempt to look at them, I just turned off my notifications and sat quietly in the room. For the first time since Shelley told me to call the ambulance, I had time to properly meditate and pray. My prayer wasn't complicated, just asking God, if it be His will, to heal and protect Shelley.

The rest of the morning and early afternoon was a blur. I hadn't slept in over thirty hours, doctors and nurses kept coming and going to check on Shelley, have me sign more paperwork, and take her for a variety of scans and tests. Shelley's family was arriving in stages, and several close friends and more distant family were down in the waiting room. We were on an ICU floor, and although they were accommodating, we were not allowed to have more than two in her room at any one time, and we were often asked to step out while they checked her EVD and busied themselves with preparation for going to surgery. Her family came down to see her one at a time as they arrived, shock and disbelief on their faces as they saw her there in the room connected to so much machinery. Finally, the surgeon came into the room and sat down with me to describe what they would be doing.

They were going to attempt to perform an endovascular coiling, a form of endovascular embolization, to block blood flow into the aneurysm. The aneurysm was a weakened area in the wall of the artery that had ruptured. Preventing blood flow into the aneurysm would help to keep it from leaking more blood. They would do this using a catheter, a long, thin tube inserted into an artery in her groin. The catheter would then be advanced into the affected brain artery where the coil would be deployed. X-rays would help guide the catheter into the artery. The coils are made of soft platinum metal, and are shaped like a spring. These coils are very small and thin, ranging in size from about twice the width of a human hair to less than one hair's width. The long-term success of endovascular coiling to treat aneurysms is about 80 to 85% and it was a procedure they used often in these matters. They would be doing this procedure in the IR, or Interventional Radiology room. Because of her condition, she was going to have to be intubated, in other words, put on a ventilator. The surgeon expected the procedure to take two to four hours once she reached the IR.

I had a couple minutes to hold her hand, her family members coming and going quickly to see her one last time. Before I knew it, she was gone, rolled somewhere deep into the hospital, and I went down to the waiting room to sit with family and friends. There were enough of us that we had taken over an entire alcove we eventually named "the apartment." There was seating for at least nine, and that was without pulling up any more chairs. The next few hours were filled with small talk, hopeful but subdued. I looked at my phone, it was full of texts and Facebook messages, hundreds of them. I read them, too distracted to answer any, but appreciative of the prayers and positive thoughts for Shelley.

Finally, around 5:00 PM, a male nurse came to the waiting room and asked to see me. Shelley was back in her room and the doctor wanted to speak with me. I followed him down to her room, the surgeon was not present, but the doctor there was definitely the one in charge. Staff scurried around him, asking questions, and getting quick answers, then whisking off to other rooms on the floor. When he saw me, he beckoned me to a computer screen and pulled up an image of Shelley's brain. It was a jumble of dark blood vessels squiggled all over the screen. He zoomed in on an area and pointed to an area that had a large blood vessel with not one bulge, but two, and what looked like a real mess all around it. He pulled a clean sheet of paper onto a clipboard and drew some illustrations on a page for me. On the left side of the page were two blood vessels with a bulge that represented an aneurysm, the second with a squiggly line showing how the platinum coils were designed to block the blood flow and repair the leak.

"Unfortunately, we were unable to fix the blood vessel. This is called a saccular aneurysm. Normally, we could seal off the bulge with the coil; however, her blood vessel was a lot different than what we expected. Once we were able to see clearly what we were dealing with, we knew the coil was not going to be an option."

He drew another picture, and this blood vessel had two bulges and some lines coming out of them.

"The blood vessel actually is bulging out on all sides. This is called a fusiform aneurysm, and it ruptured, meaning its leaking blood into the brain. We cannot treat this with the coil."

I was silent for a moment. Activity continued to buzz around us as nurses were setting up equipment all around Shelley's bed. I wasn't sure what all of this meant, but I was struck speechless. I finally managed to stammer out a sentence.

"So, what do we do now?"

The doctor set down the clipboard and went back to the computer screen. He pulled up several different images and began speaking again.

"I think we are going to turn this case over to Dr. Bhuva in the Texas Stroke Institute here at the hospital. They have already been involved in the case from the beginning, but I think they are going to have to try something a little more radical." The doctor's tone became even more serious. "Sir, your wife is very sick. She is extremely weak, and her body would not last through another surgery right now. We are going to need to give her a day or two to recover, hopefully enough that she can stabilize and regain her strength to endure another procedure. I think Friday afternoon will be the target date for surgery."

The doctor's voice droned on while my mind started racing. He was talking statistics now, ninety-nine percent of patients with this type of brain injury don't make it to the hospital, of the one percent remaining, ninety percent never make it off the operating table, and those that do are mostly severely impaired by stroke and brain damage. This last bit of information stunned me back into reality.

"Stroke damage?"

The doctor pointed to a large region of the left side of her brain which was devoid of the squiggly lines that are blood vessels.

"This area of the brain has not been getting much blood since the carotid ruptured. All the blood in the brain has caused the blood vessels to spasm shut. These vasospasms are the primary cause of stroke and the aftermath a stroke leaves behind. This side of the brain is responsible for language, number skills, reasoning, scientific skills, spoken language, and of course control of the right side of the body. Like I said before, your wife is very sick, and even if we can find a solution for the ruptured artery, we are looking at some major complications going forward. I hope you are prepared for a long stay in the hospital. The minimum recovery time in the ICU following this type of injury is twenty-one days."

I looked over at Shelley, her makeup was still perfect, and she looked like she was in a very restful sleep. There was now a ventilator doing the breathing for her, multiple drips and lines pouring medication into her body, and the EVD draining cerebrospinal fluid and blood out of her skull and into a bag. Multiple monitors tracked her vitals and a half dozen other numbers I had no understanding of. I took a moment to touch her hand and look at her, then headed back to the waiting room to fill in our anxiously waiting family.

I walked into the waiting room and all conversation stopped. I suddenly felt weak. I hadn't slept in thirty-six hours, and I had not eaten anything. Someone found me a chair. I sat down and did my best to explain what the doctor told me. I tried to be as positive as possible while conveying the seriousness of the situation. When I finished, it was very quiet. I stood up and hugged some of the family. People were murmuring quietly and for the moment, shock was the best way to describe the emotional reaction of everyone there.

"I am trying to be as positive as I can, but I think we need to also be realistic. She is in a really bad situation right now, and I believe in order for her to come out on the other side of this, it is going to take some time," I said. "I appreciate everyone being here, and want you all to know you are welcome here and in our home as long as it takes. I also don't think I have the bandwidth to be a host or worry about everyone, so please do what you feel is necessary for you, your family, and for Shelley's welfare, and if you need me, you know where I will be."

I exchanged some texts with our good friend Kyle. He had been asking what he and his wife, Jacenta, could do to help, from bringing food to driving people to and from the airport.

Wed, Apr 5 at 5:15 PM - Surgery to fix the aneurysm was not successful and they are going to keep her ventilated and sedated until Friday to try again.

OK brother, I'm having a prayer gathering for her at 6:30 in Frisco then we will stop by

How Kyle had found the time to put together a prayer gathering in less than a day was a mystery to me, but when I mentioned it to her family, Keri and her dad decided they wanted to go. It was just a few blocks down the street from the hospital. I got up and walked back down the hallway to Shelley's room. It was one of the places I would find a strange solitude; nobody talking to me or disturbing me, but a constant beeping of machines and buzzing of nurses. I sat in stunned silence for a long time and finally decided to post something else on social media to address all the people who were messaging and texting for an update.

Wed, Apr 5 at 6:28 PM - Thank you to everyone for the prayers. I've struggled with if I should update everyone on how it's going and reveal information that Shelley would want to remain private. But if we don't know what to pray for, we can't pray properly.

Today's surgery did not go as planned and was unsuccessful at repairing the aneurysm. She will remain ventilated and sedated while they drain the fluid off her brain, and then try another repair surgery on Friday at the earliest.

We need to pray for her protection until Friday, and then for her healing after that. We are looking at several weeks or more in the hospital. If you know me at all, you know where I will be. Thank you to everyone for the offers to help, it is a bit overwhelming right now, not knowing what to do, so I'm just living minute to minute waiting for my favorite person to wake up.

The next few hours were spent wandering back and forth between Shelley's ICU room, "the apartment" in the waiting room, and taking elevator rides to the coffee shop on the first floor. Everyone had advice for me:

Make sure you eat.

Get some sleep.

Go home, there is nothing you can do here.

My (fill a name or family member in the blank) had a stroke and...

Both Shelley's and my phones were vibrating constantly with messages, notifications, and texts. It was hard to concentrate long enough to return many of them. I tried to sift and filter through them to make sure I wasn't missing anything from family. Shelley's ICU room was small, and there was not a couch or foldout of any kind to sleep on. There was a reclining chair, but it was going to make staying long term uncomfortable. I saw some pictures of Kyle's prayer gathering on social media. I was surprised to see a couple dozen people there on such short notice. The prayers were very passionate and focused. By 9:30PM it was decided that most of the family would go back to our house which was about forty-five minutes away. I was torn between spending the night and going home to make sure all the farm animals were okay and prepare myself for a long-term stay at the hospital. My dad and his wife had jumped in their car early in the afternoon and were driving down from Michigan, hoping to arrive sometime the next afternoon. Back from the prayer gathering, Keri told me to go home and take care of what I needed, it was going to be marathon. She was going to tuck herself into the chair and stay in the room with her sister. I managed to stick it out until about 1:00 AM, but finally the ICU nurses kicked me out and said only one guest could stay overnight in the room.

I asked the nurse if my wife would be okay until the morning. Shelley looked stable and seemed like she was sleeping peacefully. The nurse's response was similar to what I had heard from several doctors already, and one I would hear at least two dozen more times in the days to come.

"Sir, your wife is very sick, and there is simply no way to determine how long she will be able to survive like this."

I started referring to this response as "THE ANSWER" in my mind. Substitute any gender and friend or family member to make it apply to the current situation, some sort of thing they taught in medical school. It was not reassuring.

We already had accumulated several food baskets and a cooler of drinks in the waiting room, and I checked to make sure everything was secure in "the apartment." When I arrived home about 2:00 AM, the rest of the family was already asleep, wiped out from the emotional roller coaster of the day. I walked into our master bedroom, not much longer than 24 hours since the ambulance had come to our house. It already felt like a lot longer than that. The wastebasket of vomit was still sitting in the corner by the bed, I went and dumped it out in the bathroom and started rinsing it out. Exhaustion hit like a freight train, and I left it where it was and laid down on my wife's side of the bed with my clothes and shoes still on. Her perfume was lingering on the pillow, and I drifted off to sleep with tears in my eyes, too tired to think about what would happen next.

That is my best recollection of how we got to this point. More happened in that twenty-four-hour period than at any other time in my life. Even though I had not slept in over forty hours, I found myself wide awake before dawn, staring at the ceiling, overwhelmed with guilt for leaving the hospital, and wondering what I was going to do...about anything and everything. There were no emergency messages from the hospital or Keri, so I knew my wife was still alive, that was a start. I decided the best thing for me to do was to prepare myself for a long stay at the hospital, make sure our farm animals were settled for a few days, and not lie there in bed wallowing in self-pity, but first I would start with a prayer.

"God, we need a miracle."

Sometimes I wonder if it's cliché for a person to say they are living day to day, or hour by hour. I don't feel that way anymore. After the experience of the previous day, I realized in moments of trauma, there is no other way to live. I also felt like this was going to be the only way I could get through the rest of this, no matter what the outcome.

It was still dark, not time to do the chores yet, so I decided to look at Facebook Messenger. The number of messages was surprising, and I spent over thirty minutes reading and responding to as many as I could. The sun was rising, and I needed to get my chores done before heading to the hospital, I figured I would have time to finish them up later.

I noticed right away that one of our horses, Lazarus, was looking extra thin. All our horses are rescue animals, which means they usually have some sort of issue that makes them not desirable. Lazarus is a beautifully built buckskin; with the pickiest appetite I have ever seen. He eats two things, green grass and a senior level sweet feed. We have spent thousands of dollars trying to diagnose and treat every possible cause, and the darn horse is just picky. He refuses to eat hay and just about anything else we put in front of him. It is hard to keep weight on him in the winter, and I made a note to myself that I would need to let Logann know she had to spend individual time with him helping him eat or we would lose him. I spent time with all the animals, checking feed and water levels as well as inspecting all of them, thinking about how I was going to keep everyone informed about my wife's condition. The number of messages coming in was a lot higher than I anticipated, so I decided social media would have to do. I would help everyone keep up by writing a daily update.

Thursday, April 6th – Cherry Pie Please

Day 2 - We continue to be in a holding pattern, waiting for her body to ready itself for another surgery. There has been a little talk of possibly moving it up to today, but as the afternoon wears on I am thinking it is getting too late for that.

I really am humbled by the amount of prayers, messages, and offers to help that have come to us. Let me tell you, if Shelley were awake, she would tell every single one of you to pray for someone else who needs it more. Not that she wouldn't appreciate it, but that's always been her heart. Take care of others first. The problem is, she isn't awake, and she isn't aware of the fight her body is in to stay alive. So please keep praying for her, her doctors, and our family. And if you feel so inclined, pray for the woman down the hall that just had a brain tumor removed, and everyone else on this floor that is in as much or more jeopardy than Shelley.

I have been politely declining all the offers for food. Shelley's dad said maybe I should screen the offers and if someone is offering a cherry pie with the "crust in strips" across the top, I should go ahead and let them bring it by. I can always count on Ron for a laugh, even in somber moments. But it did get me to thinking, if you are feeling driven to cook us a meal - cook one! And then take it to a family in need or maybe a shelter or homeless person. That's what Shelley would want.

For all those who are asking, beyond prayer, what can you do? Be patient. The doctors have told me this is going to be a long journey. We won't even know to what extent that is going to be until after a successful surgery.

Right now, I'm living minute to minute, praying to God to bring my wife back to me. She is my partner in all things. I like to think this outpouring of support is a reflection of how she cares for

others. I am saving every message, every text, everything for her to see, because I know as embarrassed as she will be, her heart will be full of joy to see her friends, family, and peers united in prayer.

. . . .

LOOKING BACK ON THAT post, I have no idea how I wrote that. The honest truth was that my wife was dying. Most of the day was spent watching doctors and nurses come and go, assessing her situation and trying to decide if her body could handle another surgery. Several of the doctors felt like she would not last another twenty-four hours. Yet somehow, I churned out something optimistic and positive, most likely because I couldn't bear the thought of any more eyes looking at me like those that were there in the waiting room.

There are several different types of people one begins to recognize when living on an ICU floor for a while. There is the immediate family and close friends of the patient, most have bloodshot puffy eyes and tear-stained cheeks, but they have fresh clothes, shaved faces, and combed hair. There are the more distant relatives and friends, somber looks on their faces, with flowers and gifts or food in their hands. Then there is "the one." They would be a spouse, a sibling, a parent; the one who is closest to the patient. Their faces are blank, eyes empty, no makeup, hair messy, unshaven, same clothes day to day, looking like they slept in them several nights in a row. I saw that person in the mirror every day. I also began recognizing that same individual for each patient on the floor. Shuffling around in socks at 3am looking for some ice chips and a soda, eating cold fries from a random foam container, knowing every doctor and nurse on the floor by name – sometimes even concocting nicknames for them; these were the professionals, the lifers, I would end up being one of them, and it always felt like all eyes were on us.

Then there was Ron Byrd.

Shelley's father, Ron, is a Marine Veteran. His entire life and career were dedicated to the armed forces; from serving in Vietnam to flying on Marine One, he put his life on the line for our country. He did not talk much about what he had seen, especially during the war; however, the few stories I had heard were unimaginable horrors, things that our worst nightmares are made of. Ron was a door gunner on a Huey Helicopter, and I recall him talking about reaching down to grab his friend's hand and pull him up off the ground in Vietnam in the middle of battle. When he pulled him up, all that was left was the arm he was holding on to. So, when he came to his daughter's side, he came already seeing the worst life could deal out.

Ron has found a way to cope with the bad, and it was to always find humor or positive thoughts in any situation. That doesn't mean he isn't a serious or stern man, he just saves that Marine attitude for situations that require it. Even with his daughter's life hanging by a thread in the hospital, he found a way to keep most everyone relaxed and at ease as possible, which is how I found myself in the middle of the cherry pie conversation.

"There are so many offers from people to bring food for everyone," I said to the family while sitting down in the waiting room. "It will just go to waste if we accept it all. I will probably ask people to wait for a while until we have a better idea what the next few months are going to look like."

"Now wait just a minute," Ron spoke up. "Let's talk about this for a minute. Maybe you should screen what they are offering and then we can decide if we want them to bring it or not," he joked. Well, partially joked anyway.

"What food items should I let through," I shot back at him.

"Well hold on now, let's see. We could definitely use some cherry pies, you know, the one's with the strips of crust across the top?"

We had a good laugh about that, a moment of humor in a sticky predicament. Looking back on this update, I realized something important. While I certainly didn't do it with these intentions in mind, I kept the post as positive as possible. If prayer matters, and I believe it does, the outcome could have been dramatically different if I had reported the situation differently.

If prayer matters.

If I had reported what the doctors had conveyed to me throughout the day; that Shelley was too weak for another surgery, that her numbers were all too far off the norm, that she was on entirely too much medication, and that there was very little hope of her surviving another twenty-four hours, then I think the prayers would have been radically different. They would have been for the comfort of our family, for her safe journey to be with Jesus, and any other form of surrender one can think of. I was not ready to surrender. I did not want people praying for her quick and pain-free passing.

If prayer matters.

Shelley's close friend, Rebecca Sprouse organized a prayer vigil at our church for anyone wanting to pray. A lot of people showed up and prayed for a long time. Rebecca sent me a message late in the evening.

Tonight was amazing. For some reason, Facebook was weird and didn't keep the live going and especially through the songs. Testimony's given, prayers, etc. all were powerful. Shelley would have felt them all. I have a prayer shawl and a prayer cloth that we all prayed over and anointed. I just need to meet with Pastor Jason tomorrow sometime for him to pray over them and anoint them as well. The prayer shawl has been on a few people prior who were not doing good and today they are miracles. My mom said she was told she had to give them to me for Shelley. Praying for y'all continuously.

If prayer matters.

Shelley and I also led worship on Thursday evenings at a church called The Branch. Their pastor reached out to me with a quick message.

Tim. Just found out about Shelley and we are rallying The Branch crew to pray.

If prayer matters.

The messages and prayers coming in that evening reflected my update, and in hindsight I believe that was the foundation for the miracle that we were going to witness. People were uniting to pray for recovery. This was not just the typical "thoughts and prayers." People were genuinely on their knees in prayer. I felt overwhelmed and humbled by the sheer number of people and prayer that were bringing their thoughts to bear on my wife and her recovery. The last message I read that night was from an old college friend I had not seen or spoken with in twenty years. It helped me as I fell asleep in the uncomfortable chair in Shelley's room. It really meant a lot to me that people were so deliberate in their prayers.

Tim, I just read your post. I'm praying for Shelley. Just wanted to hold space for all the fears you may have and the unknown of all you are experiencing. It's an amazing gift to find love and a true partner in life. I'm praying for your strength and miracles to bring your love back to you in full capacity as you know her. May this time of unknown just be meant for her full healing before her return to you.

Thank you. That means a lot.

Shelley and I have seen prayer work in our lives on several occasions. Shelley prayed about reopening the salon and being faced with going to jail, and she says she felt God tell her not to worry, He would protect her. He most definitely did. When she decided to run for office, we prayed together on the day when we had to make the decision if she was going to do it or not. We had no money, no hope of being able to fundraise the millions of dollars needed to compete in the race, and the prayer was a simple one. God, if you want us to do this, we need the means. Seconds after we finished that prayer, her phone rang with the news that we had a million-dollar donor. We had also learned that God would test us in those prayers, we would need to remain obedient, and that things did not always come in the timing we desired.

I had no idea what prayer was going to accomplish for Shelley in this case, and what God's will was in the matter, but I did know we had a lot of people praying, and it was up to me to help direct their energy and what to pray for.

If prayer matters.

It most certainly does, and we had a lot of it.

Friday, April 7th – The Flex Embolization Device

April 7th, 2023 - Day 3 - Shelley was in surgery from 1:45pm to 5:45pm today. The doctors feel confident they were able to repair the carotid artery properly. She is still sedated and on a ventilator. The next two weeks will be spent in the ICU as we work to get the fluid drained off the brain, monitor the progress of the surgery, and wait for her to heal enough to wake her up and wean her off the ventilator. We will not really know more about Shelley's condition until that point.

I am so appreciative of everyone's prayers and support. I am truly blown away by the number of people who have reached out. We are going to need you. This recovery is going to be a marathon. For now, her immediate family is surrounding her with love and prayer.

I have been trying to respond to everyone, because each message has been a little glimmer of hope. I am also going to try and print some of them out for Shelley so she can see them when she wakes up. She will love to see the pictures and prayers. I am deeply thankful to all of you.

• • • •

I FELT LIKE THREE DISTINCTLY different people on this day. The first one was wondering who the heck ate my breakfast when I came down from Shelley's room in the morning. I was probably a little hangry, and my frustration only intensified as I listened to a couple of family members squabbling over whether the coffee machine in our kitchen was broken or just needed to be cleaned out. There were at least six family members that I knew of staying at our house, plus a few more family and close friends coming and going, and there was still a half-washed bucket of vomit somewhere in our master bathroom. At that moment I did not care what anyone did at the house, I just was praying it would still be standing when I got home.

The second hat I was wearing for the day required me to gather all the data and feedback from the doctors, try to understand it myself, and then translate to the growing mass of people hunkered down in the waiting room "apartment." This also meant I needed to temper it for the different personalities. Some could take it straight. For others, I needed to sugarcoat the truth. Everyone deals with the trauma differently, and I had to constantly adjust my tone and demeanor with each person to be empathetic to their stress and sadness. I also had to try and figure out who should be allowed to visit, how to appreciate yet politely decline others, and still be true to what I felt like we needed at that moment.

The final card in my deck was the circus ringmaster. Remember those three incubators full of eggs? They had hatched. One usually expects a yield of around fifty percent. We hatched sixty chickens from sixty-eight eggs, the incubators looking like the old Jiffy Pop popcorn we cooked on the stove as kids. They needed a place to go to live in less than twenty-four hours. The puppies had to be delivered to their new owners, and I had a Joey, that's right a baby kangaroo, ready to be pulled from its momma's pouch. I found a way to get away from the hospital for a few hours that morning and take care of all those things except the kangaroo. That would have to wait. The salon lease was due, and I had to access Shelley's phone, banking apps, and property management website and figure it all out. Meanwhile, I was signing dozens of pages of forms in preparation for the surgery that they intended to perform that afternoon.

The chance they were going to do the surgery the day before had been crushed by ongoing issues Shelley was having. One, her body was not normalizing at all, even with the vent in her skull, her intracranial pressure was all over the map. That pressure is very dangerous and if it is too high, it can cause a traumatic brain injury. The normal range is between 7 and 15mm Hg. With the vent fully open her pressure would float around 12 and 14mm Hg, but anytime the vent was closed it would skyrocket to the high twenties. Shelley had also developed a very high fever, which was spiking near 105 degrees. She was surrounded by ice packs and had a cooling blanket underneath her, and her body was constantly shivering and shaking. Her blood pressure, which was normally low, was extremely high, however, when they tried lowering it with medication her heart rate would plummet along with her oxygen levels, so there was constant work to try and get that under control. She was also on max doses of Propofol and Fentanyl to try and keep her as calm and pain free as possible. Anytime they lowered either of those medications even a little bit, her body would begin to spasm and all her numbers would bounce around wildly.

I was skeptical when they took her after lunch to the IR, as the doctor told me if they couldn't keep her stable, they would be unable to perform the surgery. Four hours later a nurse came to the waiting room.

"Luther?"

"Yes, that is us," I replied. I expected they were going to tell us she was back in the room.

"I need you to come with me. The doctor would like to speak with you alone."

My heart sank. My brain was numb as I followed the nurse deep into the bowels of the hospital.

"Please, God, let her be alive."

I can't even begin to describe what was going through my mind. We went down a staff only elevator, through multiple security doors, and finally into a short hallway. We passed an open door where I saw my wife lying on a table, a machine straight out of a science fiction horror film wrapped around her with little arms and protrusions sticking out with multiple needle-like fingers poking into her. A doctor saw me and quickly closed the door. Oh no, I thought, she didn't make it. I was too tired to cry, too shocked to say anything, so I just kept walking.

The nurse took me into a sort of observation room with windows into the operating area. I could still see my wife lying there. There were a lot of people in the observation room, far more than I expected. The was a lot of hushed talking and murmuring. A doctor approached me as she removed her scrubs and mask and introduced herself as Dr. Bhuva. She directed me to a chair at a workstation covered with computer screens and controls. For the next fifteen minutes she showed me scans and pictures of Shelley's brain, describing the aneurysm in detail, and how normal treatment procedures were unable to fix the problem. She took me through the basics of the new technology she had decided to use to attempt to fix the carotid artery. It was called a Flex Embolization Device with Shield Technology, and it would be much later down the road that I would do some research and realize how new this technology really was. She had a model of the device about the size of a garden hose, and she showed me all the components of it and how it worked. I noticed quite a few doctors and other people were in the room with us watching silently. She explained how the device had been inserted into the brain coming all the way up through her groin, and that the device now resided inside the damaged portion of her carotid artery, connecting the healthy areas, and bypassing the hemorrhaged portion. The device itself, if accepted by the body, would become part of that carotid, forever sealing off the leak.

There was still a lot of danger ahead. She talked about the possibility of the body rejecting the device, the need to monitor for vasospasms causing the blood vessels to contract and cause ongoing strokes, and the possibility of other aneurysms occurring due to the massive trauma the brain had already experienced. Starting from today, a twenty-one-day clock would be started monitoring her brain while staying in their neuro ICU.

"She's going to be okay?" My wife was still lying on the table, looking vulnerable, it was so hard to maintain focus and composure.

The doctor didn't answer that question and instead pulled up some images on the screen. She spent the next few minutes showing me the damage to the blood vessels near and around the device, and finally settled on an area in the left side of Shelley's brain.

"Sir, the imaging here shows signs of a major stroke. The left side of her brain has not been receiving blood, and the pressure and damage to the brain appears to be severe. If your wife survives, she will most likely have some very serious complications due to the stroke. The next seven days are going to be especially crucial; we need to do everything we can to monitor and treat her for strokes that will occur from the spasming of her blood vessels. We need to take things one day at a time. I feel confident that the work we did today has fixed the leak, now we wait for her body to start to heal and do the best we can to monitor and protect her from further complications."

We talked for a few more minutes, and she gave me some printed material about the device in my wife's brain. There were still a lot of medical personnel in the observation room, staring at me, waiting for something or someone. It was eerie. I thanked the doctor, looked at my wife one last time through the windows, and then the nurse took me back to the waiting room where everyone was waiting for me. I did my best to explain everything as best I could. Finally, they wheeled Shelley back into her ICU room, all the family went in to see her one at a time and then left to go back to the house. Our friend, Rebecca, stopped by with the prayer shawl that had been prayed over by our pastor and church family.

Acts 19:11-12 says, "God did extraordinary miracles through Paul, so that even handkerchiefs and aprons that had touched him were taken to the sick, and their illnesses were cured, and the evil spirits left them."

The shawl and accompanying handkerchief had come from Israel, anointed with oils, and prayed over by many people. Little knots were tied into the strings hanging from the ends of it symbolizing the different prayers people had prayed over the shawl. I was very grateful for everyone who had a part in getting it to us. Rebecca helped me lay it over Shelley's legs and prayed for her. We visited for a short while before she left, and by 9:00PM it was just me and Shelley's sister Keri taking turns sitting with her while the other napped in the waiting room.

It had been over sixty hours since Shelley's last words, and I wondered if I would ever hear her voice again. At 11:54PM I received a message from one of our friends at church who had been a leader of the women's bible study Shelley had attended.

We are praying for all of you!!

Thank you. We miss you, Judy.

Thank you. We miss you all too. I am so sorry you are going through this.... we came back to Kings Trail a couple weeks ago.... was great to be back. Wanted to come say Hi to both of you...PLEASE!! Tell your amazing wife I am checking in on both of you!!

I saw you. Shelley wanted to come say hi, but you were swamped with people. Judy, you are one of the most spiritually strong people I have met. Thank you for your acceptance of my wife. Her spiritual journey was really impacted by you whether you knew it or not.

Thank you. I really appreciate you telling me. When you are ready, and only if you would like... I would be honored to come pray with you and Shelley. But I also understand if not.

I would like Shelley to be conscious when you come to pray. I don't know exactly why, but God just showed me that. I will keep you updated and hope you can join us when she wakes up.

I am sure some of you are asking, "What does he mean God showed him that?"

Over the past few days, I was receiving thoughts. I was not hearing or seeing words, it wasn't like that. It was more like a feeling. When our friend, Judy, sent that message about coming to pray, I felt compelled to tell her to wait for Shelley to be awake. I did not know why she was supposed to wait, I just knew that was what I needed to tell her. So, I did.

Saturday, April 8th – The Thunder of the Bikes

Day 4 - It has been a roller coaster today. Shelley's cranial pressure spiked last night and again several times this morning. We had some hope today when they tried to reduce some of the medications keeping her asleep; however, the brain is swelling and there is a fever associated with that swelling which has become problematic. So, they have maxed her medication back out and are putting in a central catheter line to give them options to address the fever. Once they have the fever beat, they will start trying to lower medication again, hopefully sometime in the next few days.

The surgeon pulled me aside this morning and told me that Shelley's aneurysm was extremely rare, and that ninety-nine percent of the people who experience it die on the way to the hospital. He said we were extremely lucky. That is truly a blessing.

Last night, a friend of ours, and someone who really helped Shelley on her spiritual walk this past year messaged me asking how I was doing. I answered, "Even though I'm not alone, I'm alone, because my best friend is locked away in her own head right now."

Today I woke up and thought about what a selfish answer that was. I'll explain. Last Sunday, Shelley led the song "You Make Me Brave" - it has become one of her favorites. I really have a hard time keeping myself together during that song. It reminds me of how she stood in front of the judge that threw her in jail, and how she will tell you that God gave her the words and courage to say what she did. I know her well enough to know that song is rattling around in her head right now, and how selfish it is for me to complain about feeling alone when she has no choice but to be where she is. I miss

my best friend. It's hard feeling so helpless. And my prayer tonight is please, Lord, make me brave for her.

• • • •

THERE ARE TWO YOUNG male doctors who look no older than their early twenties, at least to me, but that's probably because at this stage in my life I am no longer a good judge of someone's age. I have nicknamed them Doogie number one and Doogie number two, after none other than Doogie Howser. Don't get me wrong, this is not a sign of disrespect. Both these young men are geniuses at what they do. Additionally, with so many doctors and nurses around, it is hard to keep track of everyone, and nicknaming some of the more important staff helped us keep track of who was coming and going.

During the team rounds, Doogie number one pulled me aside. I had been expecting a turn for the better after the surgery the day before, but instead Shelley had suffered from increased cranial pressure, swelling of her brain, a raging fever, and vital signs that were extremely unstable including her blood pressure and heart rate. He reminded me that ninety-nine percent of the people who suffer this type of incident never even make it to the hospital, and of the remaining people that make it to the hospital, most die on the operating table or in the IR, and those who make it past that usually suffer from a severely reduced quality of life. He was very concerned about the stroke damage on the left side of her brain, as well as the inability to reduce what was becoming a life-threatening fever. He said they had decided to experiment with a central catheter, which would move cooled water through her body and try to cool her off internally. The device consisted of a cooling unit that was the size of a kitchen trash can, a bunch of hoses, a ten-inch-long metal spike, and several other smaller and less invasive parts. Unfortunately, it was rare they use these devices, and so it was taking several nurses, doctors, and a technical representative to get everything balanced and working properly.

Most of the morning and early afternoon were spent trying to stabilize Shelley; adjusting medications, trying to cool down her internal body temperature, and monitoring her brain for vasospasms that would cause another stroke.

Up to this point, other than family, a few close friends, and our pastor, nobody knew where we were. I was trying to limit visitors for the time being since Shelley was on the ICU floor and we just didn't know what was going to happen hour to hour. Our church's motorcycle ministry prayer team had been in touch with me several times wanting to come to us for prayer. Something in my spirit was tugging at me to let them come and I called the leader to let them know we would do our best to accommodate them if they wanted to ride down.

Within minutes of me hanging up the phone, every alarm in Shelley's room started sounding. Nurses and doctors were there in mere seconds. She was having a vasospasm, her blood pressure was dangerously high, her pulse rate was off the charts, her temperature was close to 105 degrees, and she was on the verge of having another stroke. No less than four pairs of hands were uncoupling all her tubes, diodes, and machines. They were taking her to the IR for an emergency surgery. One of the doctors was having me sign a stack of paperwork while the other described how they would be going up into her brain through a catheter in her groin, and using a little needle to inject medication directly into the blood vessels that were spasming closed. The entire entourage was gone in less than ten minutes, and I was left in her room by myself, wondering what had just happened. What had started out as a day filled with hope and potential had gone completely south.

I felt so alone. Shelley and I always talked about everything with one another, and I did not have that support in this situation. Out of sheer desperation, I pulled my phone out, and I texted Shelley's phone. It was 7:45PM.

Hey babe. It's been two and a half days. I miss the hell out of you. I don't know why I'm texting you, but I figure you'll see it

someday. I'm just scared, tired, sad, and just want my person back. Please come back to me. I love you.

Our pastor, Jason, had visited this morning, and as I thought about his visit, I reflected on some of his teaching, and was reminded of one of the song, You Make Me Brave, that Shelley had led the previous Sunday.

"You make me brave."

My wife was not only brave, but bold. She had obediently followed God, even when it meant being thrown in jail.

"You make me brave."

Even when faced with the greatest of adversity, she stood firm in her conviction and belief.

"You call me out beyond the shore into the waves."

She had been called into situations where she was in danger and her life was threatened, and never once doubted God's protection.

"You make me brave."

Even now, I knew she was fighting. Every doctor had tried to tell me how the odds were stacked against her, that there was little to no hope. She couldn't hear them, at least I hoped she couldn't. So, she fought on.

"You make me brave."

What was it like for her to be locked in her own head right now? I could imagine her voice singing out, no, crying out that line, "You make me brave." It was like a lifeline for her in the dark where she was lost.

"No fear can hinder now the promises you made."

If she could be so confident in God's promises to her, I needed to have that same confidence. I needed to be brave for her. So, I prayed, and this time I prayed differently. I prayed deliberately, and it was for myself.

"Lord, make me brave, for her."

I drifted off to sleep and dreamt about a situation we had found ourselves in a couple years earlier. After being released from jail by the

Supreme Court of Texas, Shelley had felt like we needed to be helping others have the courage to open their businesses and stand up for their rights. She was being invited to speak all over the country, and one weekend ended up in Hartford, Connecticut. She was speaking at a rally to help reopen the state, and it was counterprotested by a very large group of Antifa. There were at least two thousand of them, and they surrounded our group speaking on the steps of the State Capitol. We did not have private security, and there were only a handful of State Capitol police there. I was confident we were going to be severely injured and possibly even killed. It is one of the only times I can remember truly fearing for my life. I asked Shelley if she wanted to leave, not knowing if we would even be able to get past the increasingly violent crowd. She refused to be intimidated or back down, and not only went ahead with her speech, but at one point wandered into the opposing crowd to try and defuse some of them. It was on that day I realized she really believed God would protect her if she was obedient to His calling for her, and that I needed to emulate that obedience if I wanted to protect her. We finished the entire event untouched by the crowd. As I woke back up, I realized God was showing me He didn't need to make me brave for her, I just needed to be obedient to Him.

A couple of nurses rolled Shelley back into the room. The doctor had administered the medicine and her blood vessels had stopped spasming shut. She was safe for the moment. As they were going through the process of hooking her back up to all her machinery, my phone buzzed. Colby and the motorcycle ministry, along with their families were here. I was stunned when I reached the waiting room. There were at least twenty of them already in there, and more coming up in the elevator.

Everyone crammed into the waiting room with our family. After some introductions and small talk, the group circled up and began to pray. Anyone who saw us must have been shocked. Men in motorcycle jackets, many with beards hanging well down their chests, women, children, old, young, everyone in a circle praying, a few people had oil out and were putting it on the back of our necks and foreheads. The prayer time lasted for ten or fifteen minutes with several different people praying and speaking. When we finished, Colby asked if any of them would be allowed to go down and pray in Shelley's room.

Many months later, Pastor Jason would tell me how he admired the way I was guarding my garden. That phrase, "Guarding my Garden," was a title from one of his sermons. My wife was in an ICU with an open surgical vent drilled into her brain. She was vulnerable and needed to be protected. I wasn't thinking specifically about his message at that time, I was just doing my best to honor the safety and privacy of my wife.

I thought about my dream earlier in the day. God didn't need to make me brave; He had already given me the ability to be bold, I just needed to be obedient to what I felt He was telling me to do. I told Colby he could go in the room with me, and several could stay out in the hall. We went down to her room and stood on either side of her bed. The prayer shawl was over her legs, she was lying in a comfortable position, and for the moment her vitals were all at normal levels. Colby asked me if he could lay his hands on her, and I allowed him to do so.

He placed one hand on her arm and the other carefully on her forehead and prayed quietly. It was a different kind of prayer than I was used to hearing. In this prayer there was no asking "if it be Your will," instead it was a declaration of her healing and survival. The intensity of the prayer was ramping up, and I saw out of the corner of my eye that Shelley's pulse rate had quickened, her oxygen level had increased, and her blood pressure had risen but was still in a healthy range. Usually, those things were accompanied by an increase in cranial pressure and spike in fever, but neither of those things happened. In fact, her temperature dropped by a degree.

I think many of us often wonder if prayer truly makes a difference. If you haven't already figured it out from the first few chapters of this book, I believe it does. Tonight was one of those times. Undoubtedly, the words being spoken over her were having an immediate impact. I could see it on the monitor screen hanging over the hospital bed. Shelley's face was glowing, almost radiant. A little sliver of me was unrealistically hoping she was going to open her eyes and hop out of that bed. What I did see was a peaceful and relaxed countenance around her.

Colby smiled at me and said he could feel her spirit and presence, that she was going to be okay. By now her pulse was really quick, and I wondered if she could hear us. We spent a few minutes talking and then I walked Colby back to the waiting room. Some of the group was in the hallway, hands and arms outstretched, praying for Shelley, for the doctors, for the nurses, and the other patients. We all spent another half hour visiting and praying together, and then they left. Our family was emotionally exhausted from the day and started their journey back to our house, leaving Keri and I to take turns watching over Shelley throughout the night. Her vitals had quickly normalized after Colby and the prayer team had left, and I hoped we would have an uneventful night. My phone was full of messages from people praying and offering help, and I tried my best to answer everyone. Tomorrow was Easter Sunday, and as a worship leader and creative pastor for the past twenty years, I couldn't remember an Easter when I wasn't working in the church. Tomorrow would be the first time, and it would be spent here in the hospital with my wife.

Day 5 - Another day of ups and downs. The doctors finally decided to do a procedure late this afternoon to address some spasms the blood vessels in her brain were having. Overall, the surgery went well and they felt like they were able to help prevent against the possibility of a stroke. Her numbers continue to look pretty good as long as she stays sedated and medicated, but she hasn't been awake since Wednesday, and we can't keep her that way forever. So, we start the process over again of trying to reduce sedation, pain medication, and trying to stimulate her neurologically.

I'm hopeful tomorrow will be a better day. I'm thankful for where we are now, but all of us are ready for some good news without more challenges or hurdles.

I spend my time talking to her, reassuring her, and I just can't imagine what it must be like to be locked in there and unable to come out.

A good friend of ours stopped by today and prayed with us and asked specifically for her to wake up and open her eyes. I think that's a good prayer. I'll take that. I can deal with the rest. I just want her to wake up and see the love and support ready to carry her back to health.

· · · ·

THERE ARE SEVERAL ROUTINES I have become very familiar with. First, is the battery of testing and imaging done in the wee hours of the morning before the shift change. Because of the huge amount of work it takes to move her, the process starts at about 2:30AM. The nurse and an assistant spend about thirty minutes unhooking all her tubes, ports, diodes, and vents. Once that is completed, it's a race to get a CT scan, an ultrasound, an X-Ray, and get her hooked back up before her vitals swing wildly out of control. Once back in the room, they do the best they can to clean and freshen her linens and gown, untangle all the things they disconnected, and get her settled back into a comfortable state. The whole process lasts about ninety minutes and at times is very stressful as multiple alarms start beeping as we reach the threshold of time she can be safely out of her room.

Even on Easter Sunday, the hospital is operating at full capacity and several doctors are concerned with the results of the ultrasound. The blood vessels in the brain are still too constricted for the blood to flow properly and the danger of a stroke is imminent. They tried flushing her cranial cavity through her EVD with medication that is supposed to help the blood vessels relax, but it did not have the desired results.

The second routine is one of trying to reduce Shelley's medication and shut, or clamp off, her EVD. Unfortunately, that results in increased cranial pressure, elevated blood pressure, and a spike in her fever. Then it takes a while to stabilize her and get her comfortable, at which point they start the same process all over again.

Because she is not responding well to this, and because of the concern from the ultrasound, Doogie number one has decided to do another surgery this morning, going into her brain through a catheter and poking around with a needle and applying medication directly into the stressed blood vessels. This will bring the total up to five surgeries in five days. I am also starting to have some real concerns about what we are doing as a family. I texted all of them before they arrived at the hospital.

There is a lot going on here this morning, there is talk of another procedure, possibly even today. I got a lot of info from several of the doctors, and I think we need to sit down and hash out a little bit of a plan. We've all been in crisis mode, but I know everyone can't just put their lives on hold. This is going to be longer and more difficult than any of us have guessed at, so I think we

need to figure out what everyone is capable of and willing to do. Let there be no doubt I am going to take care of her to the best of my ability no matter how long or what the outcome, even if I must do it myself. So, I just want everyone here when they can today so we can all talk together.

After they took Shelley down to the IR, I texted her phone. I had some concerns about her state of mind. We hear conflicting stories about what people can hear and comprehend when in a coma. If she could hear what was going on, I was sure it would be frightening and discouraging for Shelley. I could not fathom what she would be thinking if she could hear all the different medical opinions, and I wanted her to know that I wanted her back no matter what. The texts to her phone were becoming a prayer language that I wanted to share with her. I had this feeling coming over me constantly, if I wanted or expected a miracle, I needed to be doing miraculous, or at least extraordinary things. Utilizing every form of communication available to comfort my wife was a small sacrifice to make, and it was comforting to me to know there was something tangible my wife could look at when she woke up that would reassure her about my commitment to her.

Honey, it's Easter morning and the doctors are really concerned. I know you are in there fighting. I want you back so badly. I just want you to understand that I am yours, no matter what. I want you back under any circumstances. I'll never give up on you. Don't be scared to come back to me babe. I love you.

While she was in surgery, our family and some close friends had Easter dinner in the waiting room. We had so much food, we put it all out to share with all the other families coming and going that day. There was a large cart that was covered with flowers, cards, unopened food, and beverages that had been sitting against the wall for a couple days. I wanted to move it to make room for more people, and while asking around about who it belonged to, I learned it belonged to a family that had been living there for several weeks before losing their family member. They had left everything behind when they left the hospital in shock and grief. The stark reality of our own situation became really heavy for me at that moment. Every time we felt like we made a step forward, we ended up taking two steps back, and that is no way to recover or get healthy. We wouldn't be leaving the hospital together if that trend continued.

One of our close friends, Keenan, asked what he could pray for before we ate our meal, and I said, "Pray that she wakes up."

After I received notification she was back in her room, the nurse told me they felt they were able to prevent another stroke from happening. I got to spend some time alone with her, sitting up close to her head and talking to her. I wondered if she could hear everything that's being said, doctors talking about paralysis and loss of speech, nurses concerned for her ability to survive another night, and all the other conversations going on around her. Even while speaking to her and praying with her, I feel so alone and have such a huge weight on my shoulders. I hope she doesn't feel alone.

I received this message from a church member that evening.

Hello Tim, as I read your daily updates on Shelley, I wanted to share something, it is on my heart to tell her she is not alone "in there." My mind wanders to God's presence, and that He is with her, and I can only imagine the conversations they are having without the noise of the outside world. I truly believe He is preparing her for the next great thing He has for her. My prayers are with you, I hope you find some comfort in what I have shared, and I look forward to hearing her beautiful voice praising our Lord and Savior once again at KTCC.

Thank you. Those are wise words.

Monday, April 10th – The Lost Soldier

Day 6 - I feel like a tired soldier pulling on my dirty armor for the sixth day in a row. Except there is no enemy to fight. It's a helpless feeling.

Today's procedure did not stop the spasms of the blood vessels around her brain like the doctors hoped. The evening has been really hectic as they try to find some sort of resting place of normalcy for her body. She has been shivering and not comfortable. She is still asleep and ventilated. It's been six days since she last spoke, and I miss her voice.

Today I spoke with a new friend I made in the ICU. Jim has been here with his wife a day or two longer than we have. She seems to be making a slow recovery. Toward the end of our talk, Jim told me he will never take one moment for granted again. Even a simple cup of coffee in the morning was going to be special. I feel blessed that Shelley and I enjoyed every minute together like we did, and that the night this happened we spent the evening doing what we love most, making music together.

I wish I had better news for everyone. We are all a little lost. I am hopeful tomorrow will be a better day.

• • • •

IT IS HARD TO BELIEVE how much can happen and how quickly things can swing back and forth in one day. The night had passed uneventfully and Shelley's sister, Keri, was feeling positive when she posted to Facebook in the morning.

Shelley had a great night! Thank you, Jesus!! Her vitals stayed steady and most important; her Intercranial Pressure stayed consistent! Thank you, Jesus! She is OFF propofol with little vasospasm reaction in the brain! Thank you, Jesus. I can see her eyes moving behind her closed eyelids.

Thank you, Jesus! Her temperature is controlled. Thank you, Jesus! Today will be a balancing act of keeping her blood pressure/intercranial pressure controlled as Fentanyl is reduced. I am praying for my Rockstar sister to push through this day! I pray that she is able to open her eyes and maybe begin to breathe on her own. It will be pins and needles all day and continued prayers are much appreciated as they are obviously working!!

In less than nine hours, she is at a radically different spot.

Unfortunately, things have turned south, and she had another surgery today that was proven not too successful. I can't even type thoughts anymore. Shelley is fighting with all her might. That is all I can say.

Everyone was in a dark spot and at their lowest. Every day there was another surgery. Every day our hopes were crushed a little more. There seemed to be no answer the doctors can give us. I have had to play referee with the family, people are on edge with one another. One thing I have come to understand is that people grieve or handle trauma differently, and it often causes conflicts with others close to them if the other person is processing things in a different manner. My advice has been we all love Shelley in a different way; as a mother, a father, a husband, a sister, a daughter – but we need to remember we all love Shelley.

We have adopted a lot of people into our family in the waiting room. We met Jim and his wife, Chris. Chris was having a cancerous tumor removed from her brain. Barbara and Peggy, ministers from Bakersfield, California, became close with Rachael over several days. Walking down the ICU floor, I see a lot of the same faces in all the rooms, and sometimes am surprised to stumble on an empty room, especially when just hours before the patient in the room was not in any condition to be leaving. The harsh reality is that in a Neuro ICU, a lot of the patients are fighting a losing battle long term, and in all honesty, I am worried we are about to become one of those casualties. I was at the lowest point I have been so far.

I spent the evening looking through photos and videos of my wife and I together on my phone. I am lucky to have hundreds, if not thousands of photos together with her on stage performing and attending events together. I never took any of those moments for granted, and I found myself grateful we have crammed so many amazing memories into our life together. Even so, I became angry that I might never have any more of those moments to look forward to. I switched over to social media to read some of the comments on my most recent update.

Keep your focus on Him. Do not be shaken. Your armor feels heavy and worn but it isn't. Your strength is in Jesus. He is with you. So so close. Stand on the Rock of His Faithfulness. Look toward Him like a sunflower that need the sun because their life depends on it. He's going to win this one. He will. I know it!

You, your family and Shelley I find fills my thoughts much of every day since you first posted! I am praying for her full recovery! Miracles can and do happen! It's not that much to ask for from our Creator! Or to expect!

Tim, thousands of us were praying for a miraculous turnaround today but, for reasons known only to God, that wasn't today's plan. So, we regroup and ask God to wrap his arms around Shelley and make her warm and comfortable so her body can center on healing. And we pray for you and all the family to experience God's gift of supernatural peace.

John 16:24– Ask (on my name) and you will receive that your joy be made full. Lord Jesus, King of Kings and Lord of Lords, we ask for you resurrection power to bring Shelley back to Tim, back to all of us. We KNOW you are able; you are our healer, and YOU love Shelley and Tim. Restore her health and make our joy full!

Tim don't give up. God is a miracle worker and I just know he has a lot more planned for Shelley's life. I know these 6 days have seemed. like a lifetime for you but considering what Shelley's brain has gone through it isn't that long. I know that is easy for me to say because I'm not in the situation. Asking the Lord to give the doctors wisdom to figure out how to help Shelley. I'm praying for you as you patiently wait for Shelly to wake up. Praying for Shelley's brain to heal and be able to come off the ventilator. We don't understand why we have to go through things like this, but God is in control of this situation. Thank you for the updates and I hope tomorrow is a better day.

Please add a few things to your prayers.... Tonight, tomorrow and in many days to come. Tim Georgeff needs prayers for the ability to feel God's presence surrounding him when he's feeling a bit defeated. He needs prayers to assure him God's beside him and carrying his wife through this! He needs prayers to know we are all fighting this fight with him. Thank you, my friends, for praying. Hugs

Altogether between social media, texts, and email, there were over six-hundred messages, and I read them all. It was really late by the time I finished. Shelley's daughter, Rachael, had been keeping a journal, and I read her entry, it said:

I prayed so hard this night, mama. Ugly tears, face on the floor. I prayed for your strength, and I asked Him for a little for me. It felt like He hugged me. That's when I knew everything was going to be okay.

I sat there in the dark with Shelley for a long time. The nurses did their hourly check and moved next door to their other patient. The ICU was unusually quiet, just the steady rhythmic pattern of beeps, whistles, and clicks from all the machines attached to my wife's body.

I went to her bedside and knelt down next to her. I tied a knot in one of the braids of string hanging from the prayer shawl, and I prayed out loud.

"God, give me back my wife. I don't care what the circumstances are. I don't care what obstacles we need to overcome. I just want my wife back. Wake her up and allow her to open her eyes. It is time for her to escape the darkness where she has been trapped for the last week. God, give her back to me."

I stopped. I felt angry. I wondered if this was okay, being angry with God seemed like it might not be the best choice. Names from the bible flooded into my head. Jonah, David, Moses, Jeremiah, Jacob – all had argued with or been angry with God. Another thought entered my head, He appreciated my honesty, and almost immediately I became aware of another feeling in my head in the form of a question. What did I want?

"I want my wife back," I said out loud.

The feeling was still there, pressing into me even harder, asking me to be specific. I tied another knot into the prayer shawl and prayed out loud again. This time it was short and simple. Make no mistake, I was not calm, in fact, I was almost in a panic.

"God, tomorrow I need my wife to open her eyes."

I got up and went to the couch in the room and laid down. I was so exhausted from lack of sleep the past week I drifted off to sleep almost instantly, but I clearly remember asking myself why I wanted her to open her eyes, why that was the prayer. My last thought was, it was just as much for me as it was for her. I needed something to grab onto, some sort of hope. I needed a miracle.

Tuesday, April 11th – So Close

Day 7 - Today started off hard. Her numbers were bad, scans showed signs of a stroke, and the doctors were not sounding very positive. For what seemed like the hundredth time I had to sign all the waivers and disclosures for another surgery. This time the doctors felt confident they successfully opened one of the blood vessels that had been spasmed shut. They also informed me to plan on another seven to ten days like today, trying to balance medications, monitoring and intervening on strokes and blockages, testing and more testing, and trying to find a way to bring her back out of her sleep. If we make it that far, after that everything is unknown.

But something special did happen today. After Shelley's neurological exam, everyone left the room and I spent a few minutes talking to her alone. They had not been able to get a lot of positive response from her, and she only would open her eyes when they used some physical stimulation. They were worried her hearing might be compromised and had left me feeling pretty low. As I was talking to her I told her the prayer I asked for today was a simple one: "I am just praying for you to open your eyes and wake up. Once we do that, we can start our journey back together, one step at a time. So come on babe, just open your eyes for me."

Her eyes opened. I wasn't touching her or stimulating her in any other way. Her pupils were unfocused, but she blinked, and I told her how much I loved her and that everything was going to be okay. I leaned down to kiss her forehead and when I straightened up they were closed again.

I don't know what that means. Five minutes later they were taking her for another surgery to try and open the blood vessels in her brain. She was back asleep, but for a brief moment I saw my wife

again. Later today, a friend I grew up with called to check on me and told me to never let that moment go.

I won't.

And my prayer continues, "Lord, wake her up."

• • • •

EVERY MORNING STARTED with a full neurological exam. They would reduce the medications and try to get responses to different stimuli. There was never much of a response - if any at all. Sometimes, I think we imagined seeing little twitches or movements because we wanted to believe everything was okay. One thing that always made me hopeful was that the doctors told me her pupils would respond to light when they forced her eyes open and shined their little pen light into them. Some of the harder physical things also would cause her eyelids to crack open slightly, but again we were unsure if it was an involuntary reflex or if Shelley was trying to open her eyes. There would also be hourly exams that were less extensive, none of them very promising.

This morning was a little different. The scans taken in the early morning hours had shown signs of another stroke occurring, and they had done an emergency surgery right away. This time they had to use a balloon to open a blood vessel that was spasming shut. The vasospasms were still occurring regularly from all the trauma her brain had incurred, and one of the "Doogies" told me I could expect this to continue for a while. After they brought Shelley back from the surgery, they performed their regular neurological exam, again with no real positive results.

Everyone left the room, including our family. This was becoming too much for everyone. Another surgery, another failed exam, and nothing we could see that we could latch onto for hope.

My anger from the night before had been replaced by grief. I had lost track of time, was feeling helpless, and didn't think I had the fortitude any longer to try and keep the family from imploding on itself.

I stood next to my wife's head and talked to her about all of it. I told her about how I had felt the night before, what I was praying for, how scared and lonely I was, and finally I found myself just begging her to open her eyes. I was in tears, sobbing, begging her to come back, telling her not to be afraid, that we would fight through this together one step at a time.

Her eyes opened. All the way. She blinked, and although her pupils were unfocused, I could feel her gaze on my face. I told her how much I loved her, that everything was going to be okay, kissed her forehead, and when I straightened back up, her eyes were closed again.

A couple nurses came into the room and told me they needed to take her back down to the IR. The doctors wanted to have another look at the blood vessel they had worked on early in the morning and address some other issues they had seen after reviewing her latest CT scan.

I prayed so hard during that procedure. I felt like Shelley was really close to waking up.

When they brought Shelley back, "Doogie number two" was tagging along and looked like he was about to jump out of his scrubs. When he saw Keri and I, he excitedly told us to come over to one of the computer screens and began showing us the latest angiograms. He had found a twisted blood vessel downstream from the aneurysm and opened it up with another ballon and then inserted a stent. He was positive this was the main culprit for why Shelley's brain ultrasounds and scans were not improving after the repair to her carotid.

When I told our family about what had happened, they had a bunch of questions I couldn't answer. I only knew what I had seen, had no idea what it meant, and if this was a good sign or not. I could only assume this was something positive.

It was too much, overwhelming really, and I was relieved when everyone left to go back to our house for the night. Keri said she would stay late so I could run to my dad's house in Frisco to take a shower and change clothes. I didn't have anything to change into, so I stopped at Walmart and bought myself a couple pairs of jeans and a couple tee shirts. I couldn't bear to be away long, and was back quickly. A friend of mine that I had grown up with called to check in on me. She had spent years worried about losing her husband who had battled some serious health complications. One of the things she reminded me of was to hold on to every moment, especially like the one I had experienced today. We could never really be sure if God was giving us once last glimpse.

The weight of all this was so heavy. I scrolled back through some text messages the same friend had sent me, and reread a text from April 6th.

We are all helpless in fixing this. I do not pretend to know how you feel. I just know you will be tested. And you will have more stress than you ever thought one human can endure. You're going to have family demand to tell you what they can do to help – which is not helpful. People will "help" at your house and yet leave messes everywhere. People will focus on you and not her and it will make your blood boil. It will all be too much. So make sure to be in a constant state of prayer and meditation and don't forget to breathe. Lay hands on her and pray without end. Bring in all the elders and have them lay hands...

I was so thankful for everyone. The prayers, the advice, the concern, the conversation; it all was with the best of intentions and helping me to cope, but I was also still feeling very alone. It is interesting how one can be surrounded by people wanting to help, yet feel so isolated. I texted my wife's phone before laying down on the couch.

It's late Tuesday night. You opened your eyes today. My heart was so full. I hope you could hear me. I just want you to wake up. We are so close. Come home to me honey.

Wednesday, April 12th – Wake Up

D ay 8 - Pray For Shelley to wake up!

. . . .

APRIL 12TH WAS THE most frightening day to date, and that is saying a lot considering what we had already been through. My morning routine was to be in the room at 7:00am for the shift change, see which nurses were coming on, and gather what information I could from the tests during the night. After the shift change, I had about an hour to go round up a little breakfast and check to see if anyone was down in the waiting room "apartment" before the combined stroke and neurological team made their rounds. I was caught off guard when several doctors and nurses came into the room and the head of the stroke team said, "Shut it off."

Wait a minute what?

I was confused, what were they talking about? The nurses all jumped into action and began shutting off the various drips and lines connected to her body. The cooling catheter was turned off, and her EVD drain was clamped shut.

I managed to stammer out a question, "What is going on?"

"We are going to see how she reacts to being taken off medication and support. We need to know what, if any, neurological function she has. There needs to be a reason for us to keep doing these surgeries every day. We can't just keep taking her down to the IR and utilizing our resources on a patient with no function."

The doctor's words were cold and harsh. I was in a panic. I also felt helpless. Shelley's sister, Keri, came into the room and I tried my best to explain what was happening.

"Nurse Keri," as we jokingly referred to her, had been keeping track of everything and learning all about the medications and processes

Shelley was having to endure. She knew all the nurses, knew the medication schedule, and had been in the ICU room as much as I was. Being on an ICU floor, it was two people max in the room at any time and one person spending the night. If I wasn't in the room, Keri was there. While every person played a vital role, I could not have made it through this ordeal without Keri.

We stood bedside and watched Shelley as the medication slowly wore off. I don't know what we were expecting. Unrealistically, a little part of me was hoping her eyes would pop open and she would tell me it's time to go home. Instead, we got a bunch of beeps, whistles, and alarms as her blood pressure skyrocketed, her cranial pressure went through the roof, her body temperature soared out of control, and she started fighting the ventilator. Her body was shaking and trembling, and Keri and I were holding her hands. Keri thought she saw some voluntary movement in her feet and legs. I thought I could feel her hand squeezing mine just a little bit. The doctor started her exam, and this time Shelley opened her eyes to verbal commands. That was it, there was no big movement, no recognition, but there was apparently enough, because the doctor ordered the nurses to turn back on all the machinery and said she would be back with the entire team during rounds to modify and continue the treatment plan.

I texted our family in a group chat.

We had a long night. They decided to go ahead and drop her meds and she was fighting her ventilator and definitely feeling some withdrawal symptoms, plus her blood pressure was up and down as they changed medication levels. This morning she opened her eyes several times, and she squeezed my hand with her right hand which is great news because the stroke area they are worried about is in the left portion of the brain. They are continuing to try different levels of testing as she comes further off the meds. They are adding some new monitors and medication, yay more wires, but after a tough night, I feel like the morning is starting off a little better. Waiting

on the stroke team to show up with their plan on the morning rounds.

By the time everyone reached the hospital, it had been decided there were not going to be any procedures planned for the day. Shelley was back under in a medically induced sleep as they worked on balancing medication, keeping her temperature down and monitoring the EVD. I decided I needed to get home for a little while and check on the animals, pay some bills, and generally make sure everything was still standing.

The house seemed foreign to me. In a week's time everything seemed different. Someone had cleaned the vomit out of the trash can, and there was a fresh pecan pie in the refrigerator along with what looked to be a dozen sliced brisket sandwiches from Buc-ee's, multiple bags of leftover Whataburger, Chicken Express, and multiple containers of different casseroles, leftover Easter food, and no less than six fried cherry pies.

There was some loud peeping coming from our dining room, and when I walked in, I found close to sixty baby chickens in a six-foot-long brooder with two heat lamps. I had forgotten about them, but luckily the family had figured out what to do with them and they looked pretty content for now.

Outside, the animals all seemed to be in decent shape. Not counting the sixty baby chicks, we had another sixty animals on the farm including seven horses, three miniature horses, one miniature mule, two longhorn cattle, three pigs, a dozen goats, three kangaroos, three miniature dachshunds, two great Pyrenees, and two dozen full grown chickens. Shelley's daughters had done a fine job of keeping them fed and watered, and all of them appeared healthy. I smiled at our little miniature mule, who happened to be named Doogie, after his father, a miniature donkey we had called Doug. He was letting a butterfly land on his nose and was staring at it cross-eyed, trying to figure out what to do with it.

The grass was greening up, the trees were budding and full of leaves, it was mild, and we were going to have another one of the stunning sunsets that we enjoyed so often at our place. It reminded me of a song by Andy Griggs named If Heaven. Some of the lyrics were especially poignant.

If Heaven was an hour, it would be twilight, when the fireflies start their dancing on the lawn.

We typically had fireflies all through the summer and Shelley and I enjoyed sitting on our front porch swing watching their little lights glow all over the front yard. Our property was quiet, peaceful, and our little slice of heaven.

If Heaven was a pie, it would be cherry, cool and sweet, and heavy on the tongue. And just one bite would satisfy your hunger, and there'd always be enough for everyone.

Cherry pie again. I smiled; we definitely had enough pie in the fridge for everyone right now.

And if Heaven was a tear, it'd be my last one, and you'd be in my arms again.

I sure did miss my wife.

What happened next requires me to go back in time a bit to put this into context. In January of 2008, the afternoon after my mom's funeral, I was sitting in a chair in the sunroom of my parent's house. The sun was shining, it was warm, I was mentally fatigued, and I was sitting there with my eyes closed, thinking about nothing and everything at the same time. I vividly remember the sun on my face being blocked momentarily, like a shadow passing in front of my face. I felt an embrace, almost like a hug, and the words or thought materialized in my head, "Everything will be okay." When I opened my eyes, nobody was there, the sun was shining through the skylight and there wasn't a cloud anywhere. I knew I had not been sleeping, and the experience all felt very real.

Up until this moment, I had always assumed it was my mom, that her spirit had somehow wanted to give me that reassurance.

Now, sitting in my UTV (Utility Terrain Vehicle) out in our pasture, I closed my eyes and let the sunlight warm my face. I sat there for a minute and felt a shadow pass across my face. I did not feel the same embrace I had felt in my parent's sunroom; however, the hair on my arms stood straight up and I felt a tingle go up and down my spine. Just like in 2008, I could feel the thoughts in my head, like unspoken words that just materialized in my mind, "Everything will be okay. What is it that you want?" The sunlight was back warming my face, and like I suspected there was nothing around and not a cloud in the sky. I pulled my phone out and texted my wife's phone.

I feel optimistic today, like you are gathering yourself up to fight your way out. I had to leave the hospital for a couple hours to take care of animals, bills...and everything was so beautiful at home, like it's just waiting for you to be here. Everything is green, the animals are fattening up, it was sunny and warm and a butterfly was trying to land on Doogie's nose. I miss you and want you with me here now. I know it's selfish and I don't really care. I feel guilty being away from you, but things have to be kept in order for your return. I love you and will be back at your side in a little bit.

I sat there for a while considering what had happened, and the similarities of what I had experienced in my parent's house. Shelley and I were no strangers to the feeling of being led by God. When she told me we were going to reopen the salon against the Covid ordinances, she told me that she had a strong feeling or suggestion from God that we would be protected. Even when facing one-hundred and eighty days in jail, she respectfully stood up to the judge and told me later that God was giving her the courage to stand. When we felt we had no financial option or way to pursue a seat in politics, we received a phone call within seconds of finishing a prayer giving us news we were receiving a one-million-dollar donation. We also knew that these blessings came with trials and refinement that would test us, and remaining obedient was always the best way forward.

I didn't fully understand the trial we were enduring right now, but I suddenly had the confidence that God was hearing my prayers, hearing the prayers of our family and friends, and the prayers of thousands of people all over the world. I also came to the realization He had spoken to me in 2008, He was speaking to me now, and that part of the refinement process He was expecting from me was to be more specific in my prayer.

I finished my chores out on the farm, ate dinner with my dad, his wife, and my son, and prepared to head back to the hospital. But before I left, we ate that entire pecan pie. Ron Byrd was not going to be too happy about that! When I arrived, I went straight to her room, walked to her bedside, knelt down next to her head and spoke to her.

"Honey, it's time for you to wake up. We are all praying for that, thousands of us. I know you are in there fighting to come out. I am here. Your family is here. All we need is for you to come back."

Shelley's eyes opened. This time I could see them trying to focus. She saw my face and her whole body wiggled around. Keri was out of the chair like a rocket. Shelley's eyes shifted to her, and I could see her lips try to curl into a smile around the ventilator. We spent the next half hour squeezing her hands, talking to her, watching her as her eyes would open for a minute or two at a time and try to focus on us. Sometimes her hands would feebly squeeze back, and we could see her straining to move her legs, which moved ever so slightly. She finally exhausted herself and fell back asleep.

Keri and I talked for a while and then I checked messages. I had one that stood out to me that I read several times.

Tim, I met you all when you came to Abilene and spoke. I am a retired Respiratory therapist. I want to tell you two stories to keep your hope. I dated a man for several years. He was in Houston and had a hemorrhagic stroke. Only 6-10% survive. He survived. I could tell you many stories of what I prayed, did, etc. but God moved mightily. It was a difficult recovery, but he was able to make it through it. I also had two patients during my time working at Medical City that had brain bleeds with increased cranial pressure and tubes inserted and they came through! Many of us are praying, believing, and asking God to work a miracle! The enemy hates your testimony but God...Please be encouraged and never stop loving, staying by her side and don't stop praying and believing. I know because the love of my life survived it.

There was a video of pastor Rafael Cruz praying for Shelley that I had gotten a glimpse of earlier in the day. I found it and watched it several times. We have always had a deep appreciation for the Cruz family. When Shelley was sent to jail, I received a call from their family within hours of her incarceration, and Rafael prayed for me specifically on the phone. His son, Senator Ted Cruz, came to the salon when Shelley was released and spent time talking with us. The family had always been supportive, offered good advice, and been spiritually impactful on us. I placed my phone by Shelley's head and let her hear the prayer several times. Pastor Cruz declared her to be fully healed. I prayed Shelley heard that prayer and recognized we were all waiting for her return.

Thursday, April 13th – Marvelous Light

Day 9 - My update yesterday was intentionally short, simply to pray for her to wake up. Today my update is intentionally early. Keep praying that same prayer.

Trying to bring Shelley out of her sleep has been extremely hard. Every attempt to move her that direction with medication has been met with increased cranial swelling, radically shifting blood pressure, and spasming blood vessels that threaten more stroke damage than has already occurred. She is still on a ventilator, and multiple other pumps and machines. The simple task of taking her for a CT scan is an hour of prep time, going to the scan, and an hour getting her reset after. That makes even a simple test a life threatening and dangerous situation. So, if you are praying today, let's be specific: "Lord, give her the strength to find her way out of the darkness and into the light. Give the doctors the ability and knowledge to guide her there safely and comfortably."

I do my best to try and answer everyone, and I am doing a horrible job. I appreciate everyone's prayers, support, offers to help, and desire to visit. I need all of it, we need all of it, and I will ask and inform everyone as the appropriate time comes. Shelley's condition is very severe, and her brain is exposed multiple times a day to different procedures, so we are trying to minimize contact and visits while we go through this portion of her treatment. As of now, we are blessed that our entire family is here, and they have done an incredible job of helping with the farm, home, and hospital. A few close friends have helped us with some food and close up prayer and moral support, and I can't thank them enough.

But this is far from over, and as time goes on, we will need help. I have no idea what our life is going to be like on the other side of this. Although my ultimate prayer is for her to be fully restored, my

current prayer remains the same, bring her back to me, and let us start the journey to recovery together, one step at a time.

• • • •

THE NIGHT FOR SHELLEY had passed as one of the most uneventful we had seen so far. No emergency surgeries, no major alarms going off, cranial pressure numbers staying steady. She also still was running a terrible fever that the internal cooling catheter could barely keep up with. I wandered the ICU most of the night, unable to sleep. One of the patients who had seemed to be recovering well had passed away during the night, a major code blue called out in middle of the night that had caused the entire ICU to swing into action. My phone was also melting down from the number of people who wanted a "real update." My intentionally short update the day before had left a lot of people with more questions than answers, so I posted to social media intentionally early, hoping it would slow the pinging of my phone down from its frantic pace.

Shelley was barely conscious, and I constantly wondered if she could hear what the doctors and nurses were talking about, if she heard me and her family talking with her, or the occasional visitor we allowed into the room. At one point, a financial advisor from the hospital came bustling into the room to inform me what an enormous amount of money was being expended on Shelley. She was loud and inconsiderate, and I had to restrain my anger with her when I finally got her out into the hallway and asked her not to have these kinds of conversations in front of my wife who was fighting for her life.

I was becoming increasingly frustrated with life in the hospital. The routine was slow, sleep was nearly impossible to get, and my diet was horrible. People were constantly advising me to leave, to go get sleep, or to simply take a break. There were several reasons I couldn't bring myself to do that.

First, when I did try to leave to do anything, I was constantly getting called back and told to return to sign paperwork, approve an emergency surgery, or that she was struggling and in danger.

Second, there was no way I wanted to miss the moment she woke up.

Third, there was no way I wanted to be gone if she passed.

There is one thing in my life I will never regret. I was in the hospital room with my father when my mom passed away. I saw her take her last breath. It was one of the most heartbreaking moments in my life, but also a moment a son would never want to miss with his mother, or a husband with his wife.

My dad, Craig Georgeff, has always been a larger-than-life figure for me. Maybe a lot of fathers are like that for their children, maybe not. All I know is my dad was my rock. A lifelong federal agent, he seemed superhuman to me at times. Here was a man who sometimes protected The President of the United States during the day, and coached my little league baseball team in the evenings. He investigated horrible crimes and criminals, yet found time to take me to music lessons. Late for school? "Hey son, throw the bubble on top of the car and I'll turn on the siren and get you there in time."

My dad and his wife had been coming to the hospital every day since he had arrived. They had taken it upon themselves to make sure my son was getting everything he needed while I was at the hospital, and I often found them sitting on their own in the waiting room long after the rest of the family left, just to see if I needed anything. It was also my dad who finally gave me some advice.

"Everyone else, including me is going to tell you what to do. They are going to tell you to go home, to get sleep, and to take care of yourself. I know how I felt when your mother was in the hospital. Everyone else with advice could go blow hot air somewhere else. You do whatever you feel you need to do and tell everyone else what you need them to do, including me."

It was that advice that kept me from succumbing to the overwhelming pressure to open the gates and let everyone come. "Guarding my Garden," remember? Shelley was in an ICU because her brain was exposed to the environment multiple times a day. Several times a day her EVD was used to flush medication through her brain, and keeping the area around her sterile was of upmost importance. Her vitals were critical, and she was very sick. A constant stream of visitors was not going to help her. That advice was also what convinced me I was going to stay at the hospital as much as I could. We were blessed that our friends Kyle and Mark had started a donation portal for people to help us out. As musicians, our income was mostly dependent on working gigs, and obviously Shelley was not able to do that, and if I wanted to stay with her, neither could I. Nine days in the hospital and we had already missed six shows. I also had no idea how long we would be here, what Shelley's recovery was going to be like, and what life would be like on the other side of this. People were being so generous already; it was truly humbling.

I decided it was time to start contacting people about cancelling upcoming shows. Everyone was tremendously gracious and understanding. I kept a couple ticketed events on the calendar, they were already nearly sold out, and I hoped Shelley was in better shape by then. Looking at my schedule, I also realized we were going to miss out on seeing a favorite of ours, Travis Tritt, the next night. I had purchased those tickets for her as a gift.

Mark and Kyle stopped by to tell me about a prayer gathering that had occurred at Redemption Point Alliance Church. I was still overwhelmed by the number of people that were gathering and praying for Shelley. There was even a Facebook group called Prayer Chain for Shelley Luther that had over five-hundred members posting prayers and devotionals daily.

I also started to notice that there was an increasing number of messages coming to me that were testimonials.

Tim, my heart breaks for what you are currently going through. I can attest to your circumstance though - our Lord provides and is everything we need. My brother had a motorcycle wreck in 2019. Similar to your situation, he was placed in ICU and sedated in a coma. My Family stayed w/ him every second of that time. It was heartbreaking and so frustrating to see doctors "experiment" w/ the right medication to bring Britt back. During one failed attempt, my brother awoke, and his heart rate was so high I thought he was going to have a stroke. But God......God provides - past, present, and future. The good Lord brought him back. Since doing so, our Savior changed his life: he now lives for the Lord; he was reacquainted to an old high school girlfriend who he married and had a baby boy w/; and he has a new job. Glory to the Lord; it is because of Him!!! I pray this victory gives you strength. Our Lord is always there for us. I believe your wife is going to walk away from this w/ a whole new level of a testimony. May the Holy Spirit strengthen you during this time. In the Name of the Lord, Tim, I pray for your wife's full recovery. God, please restore her. Please touch the Family; Lord God Almighty comfort them during these painful moments. Heavenly Father, touch the doctors. Lord God, we know You are the Master Physician; mankind is so limited. We pray You are w/ the medical staff though; anoint their hands; sharpen their minds. Lord God, please move like only You can. We give You the praise, glory, and honor forever, Lord. In Jesus's Name, Amen.

This message triggered a memory of Shelley. Recently, we were leaving the house and had only driven a couple of miles before coming to the scene of an accident between a motorcycle and an eighteen-wheeler. The motorcycle rider was lying under the semi. The driver of the semi was sitting in his cab in shock, and several motorists had pulled over and were all just staring at the man lying on the ground. He was writhing around on the pavement, one arm badly shattered with bone sticking out through his sleeve, and something looked wrong with his chest. I couldn't figure out why there wasn't anyone trying to help him until I saw the colors on his motorcycle jacket. He belonged to a dangerous club, and the bystanders feared him. I was able to ascertain that someone had called 911, and turned to find Shelley sitting under the semi with him, cradling his head in her arms, having helped him remove his helmet. She told me to find his phone, and I was able to get it out of his vest pocket. She grabbed it from me, put it in front of his face to get it to open, and scrolled through his contacts until she found "mom." She called her and told her what was going on, assured her we would be there with her son until help arrived, and then hung up the phone. The man was gasping for air and telling us he couldn't breathe. There was gurgling in his lungs, I could tell he was bleeding internally. Shelley had me carefully unzip his vest but told him we couldn't move him more than that in case his back was broken. He was in horrible pain, but calmed down when he realized Shelley was doing her best to save him. I was still amazed that nobody else wanted to help. EMS finally arrived, including a helicopter, and they finally loaded him up to send him to the hospital. Shelley used his phone one more time to call his mom after confirming where they were taking him, then we went home. She was visibly shaken.

After a few minutes she finally turned to me and said, "I didn't ask him if he knew Jesus."

I struggled with an appropriate reply, then finally lamely asked, "Why?"

"Because I wasn't sure what to say if he said no." She was in tears.

Later in a conversation with our pastor, he mentioned that God would give her the words she needed in a time like that, and the next time she would be ready. Don't be afraid to start that conversation.

This was a woman with work to do. God had a plan for her. He was refining her, and most likely us for something. We just needed to find a way for her to survive.

That night the prayer was extremely simple and direct. "Lord, it's time for Shelley to step out into Your marvelous light."

My text to Shelley's phone that night was also simple.

Today has been a much better day for us. You are waking up. But I know it's miserable for you. I keep trying to comfort you and explain what's going on the best I can. I hope I am helping. I love you.

Friday, April 14th - Extubated

Day 10 - It is honestly hard to believe it has only been ten days. Seems like forever ago that the ambulance came to our house. I have been hesitant to post over the past twenty-four hours because the level of uncertainty is always so high. Every hour something different is happening, another alarm is going off, another doctor is coming into the room; and we just don't know for sure if we are making progress, until today.

Our specific prayer for Shelley to wake up has been answered. She is able to open her eyes and recognize faces. She makes some facial expressions, probably wondering why we are all standing there staring at her. They were able to remove her vent tube late this afternoon. This is a huge relief, and an answer to many prayers.

We still have a long way to go. Her brain has been damaged by the cranial pressure as well as from strokes she suffered after the hemorrhage. To what extent, we still don't know. A lot of her vital signs are still up and down and need to stabilize. The EVD is still draining, relieving pressure inside her cranial cavity, and it will remain doing so for a while.

Thank you to everyone who has been praying, and I really believe being specific about what we were asking for was answered. So, what's next? I'm praying for her internal cranial pressure to normalize. This will allow them to remove the EVD, move her out of the ICU, and reduce the risk of more strokes.

Today has been a huge blessing and I am feeling hopeful. We are still in an immediate family only situation for visiting, I'll let you know when that changes. In the meantime, keep the prayers coming. They are working!

. . . .

SHELLEY FOOLED ALL of us today. She seemed stable, sleepy, and acted like nothing was going to change for the next 24-48 hours. Her fever was still extremely high - near 103 degrees, her heart rate was high - staying over 110 BPM consistently, and her cranial pressure was bouncing around. We assumed there would be no change in her status. I decided I needed to catch up on bills at the salon, feed and check on the animals at the farm, and find some clean clothes. I felt as if I had been rolling around in the same couple outfits for a week.

I had been gone less than an hour when I got a call from her daughter, Rachael, telling me her tube was out. It took me a few seconds to realize she meant they had pulled the ventilator tube out, on purpose! Not only was she extubated, but she was awake and asking where I was.

The drive back to hospital felt excruciatingly long. When I got back to her room, Shelley was still awake and trying to talk a little bit. Her voice was not much more than a severely raspy whisper, and most of what she was saying didn't make sense, but she was awake and talking!

Keri was supposed to fly out the day before to go check on a few things at home before coming right back, but her flight had been cancelled due to bad weather, so she was still at the hospital and able to speak with her sister for a moment. She also was able to talk with me and one of the "Doogies" as he showed us the most recent CT scans.

"This area here is showing all the typical signs of stroke damage." He was circling an area on the left side of Shelley's brain that was devoid of any blood vessels. "The left side of the brain controls speech, comprehension, arithmetic, writing, and of course motor control of the right side of her body. Obviously, she is talking a little bit which is a good sign, and the brain has amazing abilities to rewire itself, but realistically we need to be prepared for some large deficiencies to the physical abilities of the right side of her body as well as the ability to communicate and understand effectively."

I knew what he was saying was not totally untrue, Shelley's movements were mostly made with the left side of her body, and I had noticed the right side of her face seemed sluggish. I was also positive I had seen and felt her move the right side of her body.

He showed us another scan, this one of the area where the aneurysm had occurred. It was a big mess of swollen twisted blood vessels, a big dark object which he identified as the flex embolization device, and finally the blood vessel held open by the stent.

"We still have a lot of concern about this area of the brain. We are watching for leaking, possible rejection of the implants, and still monitoring for vasospasms."

He spent a few more minutes discussing how we were out of the first major danger zone, but that Shelley still had some major hurdles to overcome, one being getting her cranial pressure stabilized, getting her fever to come down, and to start weaning her off the pain medication. She was still maxed out on that.

We had a family meeting and discussed what our plans were going to be. Keri needed to go back to Florida for a few days. Shelley's sister, Tracy, needed to go back home for a bit, Mom and Dad would take turns, both of Shelley's daughters were staying, and my dad and his wife were staying.

I realized what a support mechanism the family had been, and felt a bit nervous with people coming and going. I also understood that everyone could not put their lives on pause forever. This was going to be a situation that ultimately Shelley and I would have to navigate together.

With both sisters getting ready to leave, they wanted to spend time in the room with Shelley, and although we were constantly breaking the no more than two people in the room at a time rule, I decided it was a little crowded and went with my dad, his wife, and my son to get an early dinner at a nearby restaurant. We had barely sat down when a stranger approached me and asked if she could pray for me.

"I know you don't know me, but I have been following you and your wife's story on Facebook. I know you need God's strength right now. You are not in this alone."

As if one nudge wasn't enough, my phone was full of reassuring messages.

I'm sure you're flooded with tons of messages. I'm praying daily for her and your whole family. God is on your side and taking care of her. Thank you for keeping us updated. Much love to both of you. Stay strong and have faith.

I also had a message from Pastor Chris at The Branch, the church where Shelley and I assisted leading worship on Thursday nights.

We devoted a portion of our service last night to praying for her. Love you both!

Saturday, April 15th – Feeding Tube

Day 11 - Another positive day. Shelley spent several hours awake, even smiling a couple times at her family. I did have to referee a wrestling match between her and three nurses attempting to put a feeding tube in her nose; however, after that surprising show of strength, I would like to think that is a positive sign of her brain rebuilding its damaged network.

The prayer remains the same: normalize and balance her internal cranial pressure. That will help stabilize a lot of the other issues that she is still fighting with. After so many days of what seemed to be a constant stream of negative news, I'm very cautiously optimistic that we are making sustained progress.

I think we might be the "senior" family on the floor now, meaning we have been here longer than the rest of the patients. I have seen some leave that were healed, and I have seen some leave having moved on to be with Jesus. I am relieved we are still in this and fighting hard.

We are so thankful for everyone who continues to lift Shelley up in prayer, and feel blessed to have so many friends looking out for her. I know she will want to see you when she is ready.

Well, it's another night in the ICU falling asleep to the chirps, whistles, and beeps of what seems to be two dozen machines surrounding her bed. Good night!

• • • •

IT HAD BEEN ELEVEN days since Shelley had eaten anything or been given anything other than IV fluids. She was extremely skinny, and we were all worried about her nutrition level. The doctors decided they would put a feeding tube through her nose and down into her stomach. She was still sleeping when the nurses came in to do it. One of the nurses asked if she needed to be restrained and the other nurse said not to worry about it, and do the insertion from her right side since it was mostly paralyzed.

They got set up with the tools they needed and the scanner watching her chest and stomach cavity to make sure the tube made it into her stomach. The nurse began working the tube into her nose and reached the point of resistance that he needed to push through. Shelley had not moved around or responded much, yet. Even when they told her they were putting in a feeding tube her eyes had barely opened.

The nurse applied some pressure to the tube, and it began to slide past the resistance. Shelley's right arm shot up and grabbed the nurse by the neck.

"Stop it, you're hurting me," she rasped out in a throaty growl.

The nurse was so surprised he stepped back and let go of the tube. Shelley pulled it out of her nose and glared at him fiercely. It all happened so fast it took me a minute to realize she had used her right arm and hand, the side that was supposed to be impacted by the stroke.

I began talking excitedly to the other nurse, Juan. He was equally surprised, and it took them a minute to find the restraints. Shelley was belligerent and upset about being restrained and getting the tube shoved down her throat through her nose. The next several hours were spent trying to keep her from pulling it out, explaining to her repeatedly why she had it, and trying to keep her from picking at the bandage that held it in place. Finally, in the evening, the nurses decided she would need a twenty-four-hour patient observer in place to make sure she didn't pull out her feeding tube, her EVD, or any of the half dozen lines going into her body.

Shelley was more awake and aware today than at any point so far, and she was constantly wanting to talk with whomever was in the room. A lot of it didn't make sense. Sometimes I could understand what she was meaning to say or trying to convey, but it took a lot of listening, and asking her to repeat herself, which frustrated the heck out of her. But she was smiling a lot and that was what was important.

There had been some times throughout the day Shelley couldn't remember who I was. I was bending over to give her a kiss before leaving the room and she asked me what I thought I was doing, and that I needed to ask her boyfriend permission before giving her a kiss. My concern was reflected in my text to her phone.

It's Saturday night and I'm feeling a little frightened. You don't always know me. Maybe it's the medication, maybe it's just your brain re-wiring itself a little bit. And I'm probably being selfish. You are awake and talking and I have missed you for so long and I'm scared you might have memory loss. I am hoping it's the medication and we can have a good laugh about this: you called me cocky for wanting to sleep on the couch next to you. ANYWAYS, I am still thankful you are awake. I miss you honey.

Adding to the chaos that was developing around us, several news outlets and media stations had begun poking around to try and get some scoop. I had only talked with one, Mark Davis, a talk show host on Dallas radio. The only reason I talked to him was because he seemed genuinely concerned, not just trying to report a story, and several people had sent me recordings of him praying with his audience for Shelley on air. I had been unable to listen to his show for nearly two weeks, but prior to the incident had been a regular listener. I really was grateful for how he handled the situation. He even invited his entire audience to join the Facebook prayer chain that had been started by our friend Rebecca. Anytime I was feeling down, I simply had to open that page and there were dozens of prayers being added daily by people from all over the country. One especially hit me hard this day.

Dear Heavenly Father, as another day comes to a close, we thank You for LIFE and all the mighty things You've done today! Thank You for keeping Shelley AWAKE for several hours and for the physical and mental strength she displayed wrestling with the nurses! God, thank You for safely guiding Shelley out of the darkness and into the light where she can see and experience the love from Tim and their Family who surround her. We pray You would use those simple yet deeply meaningful interactions with each other to help aid in Shelley's healing process in every way possible. Jesus, we thank You for Your presence in and WITH Shelley; watching over her, every moment of every day, and we pray she would sense Your presence constantly—comforting, reassuring, strengthening, and giving her deep peace.

Lord, we pray You would extend your grace to Shelley, Tim, and whoever else is staying with them in the hospital room tonight, by supernaturally blocking out the noises of all the machines in the room so they could receive the rest they so desperately need. We thank You, Lord, for the daily strength You've provided to bring them all this far, and we KNOW You will continue! Thank You, Lord, for Your GREAT faithfulness!

We pray now, that You would do ALL that is necessary to bring Shelley through this traumatic ordeal and into COMPLETE healing. We ask, with outstretched and prayerful hands over Shelley's head, as we stand in agreement with Tim, Lord, that You would normalize and balance Shelley's internal cranial pressure and stabilize all other issues she's experiencing in her body, in Jesus' Name. Lord, we BELIEVE and PROCLAIM Your word from Philippians over Shelley that being confident of this, that YOU who began a good work in Shelley WILL carry it on to COMPLETION until the day of Christ Jesus.

Lord, You gave these words to me yesterday: Shelley is a woman of RESCUE.

You created her that way on purpose! God, You rescued her from sin and death through the death and victorious resurrection of Your Son Jesus. You rescued her from this aneurysm, placed her in the mere 1 percentile, and provided a way out of the darkness and into the light, on purpose! And You are continuing to rescue her into full and complete health and vitality, on purpose and FOR a purpose! We believe for and proclaim that over Shelley, in Jesus' Name. And we thank You for what You're going to do to bring this to completion.

And Lord, we do also pray for the families Tim referenced in his update tonight whose stories are now very, very different. Jesus, please minister to those families in ways that only You can. Comfort them deeply and provide for their every need, in Jesus' Name.

Please give rest to the surgeons and hospital staff tonight as well, Lord. And to each and every prayer warrior and family represented in this group who may need to sleep. Thank you for Rebecca and for placing it on her heart to start this prayer chain! Thank You also for Tim who so faithfully keeps us updated so we can pray specifically. We thank You, God, for depositing Your Holy Spirit power within us and for partnering with us in the POWER of prayer! May Your Mighty Name be glorified to the ends of the earth, in Jesus' Name.

This really got me wondering. If we were going to pull through this, what was the purpose? What did God have in mind for Shelley? For me? This period of refinement was intense. What could He possibly be preparing us for?

Day 12 - The message I received today said: "Why do you keep making posts about your wife like she's the most important person in the world or something?" It went on with a couple choice adjectives and some other pointless comments. But it did make me think for a while, why am I making these posts?

I know she isn't the only person that's sick. This floor we are on is filled with patients that have brain injuries. They have spouses, friends and families that care about them too. I am well aware that other families are facing uncertain futures or life-changing events. I know my wife isn't the most important person in the world, but she is the most important person in MY world, and I am hopeful that someday she will read these posts and look at the thousands of prayers, overwhelming support, and countless friends and family that were her champions. And just maybe, someday, somewhere, somebody who is praying for a miracle will be able to see anything is possible.

Last night and today have been a very slow and steady day of minuscule improvements. A little more talking, a little more movement, and along with that the challenge of Shelley becoming more aware of the situation and circumstances. ICU delirium is very real, and I can't even begin to imagine what she is thinking and feeling throughout the day.

I keep praying for her memory to improve and for the circuits in her brain to continue to repair themselves and create new pathways. I pray for continued building of strength and for the suppression and removal of the fear and anxiety that comes with the struggle to move.

I am thankful for every one of you. Our journey is really just beginning, and your support has been a true blessing.

• • • •

A LOT OF PEOPLE HATE me and my wife. That may sound extreme, but if you can imagine an outsider's perspective, here is a couple that spends much of their time on stage performing music. We already seem like we are seeking the spotlight, which is exactly what performers are supposed to be doing! Being a working performer is all about creating the perception that we are the best and biggest act to ever hit that stage.

Then my wife decides to buck the system and fight back against the Covid mandates. She is thrown in jail and made into an international hero. Every television and radio station, every news outlet, every podcast; there were our faces and some version of the story about how she was fighting for all our freedoms and liberty. She ran for state office twice, and politics, a lot like music, is about self-promotion.

Now, faced with a medical emergency, her story has been shared all over the world, and it generates just as much hate as it does love and support. Politics, jealousy, untruths, and imperceptions fuel people's feelings and create the need in them to send something negative to me.

It did cause me to do a self-check. Why was I writing these updates?

First, it was my therapy. There was simply no way I could get through every day without releasing some sort of steam. It helped me to get my feelings out and to be able to breathe a little easier. So, why on social media?

Second, it was the only way to keep everyone informed. I simply did not have the bandwidth to text and message every person that had questions or wanted detailed information. Plus, the positive feedback I was getting back, the prayers and support messages, they were helping to rejuvenate and sustain me.

Third, I was hoping it would be something Shelley could go back to someday, to look at the posts and the responses. The prayers and testimonies people shared were amazing. I was also starting to realize the need to document what was happening. If we were witnessing a miracle, I wanted to be able to accurately provide our testimony in the future.

Finally, I hoped that if someone else found themselves needing a miracle, they could look back at his experience and know God was still in the business of making them.

I understood what this specific person was trying to say, they were asking me why I thought Shelley was more important than anyone else? Simple, she was and is more important to me than anyone else.

One message of support did stand out to me that day.

Just some encouragement in response to your recent post: Never feel like you need to defend the God-given instincts to want to be that warrior He created you to be. The instinct to pray for your wife, to protect her, to call upon God, day and night, with guttural screams for healing and relief and to focus on her and her alone. It's beautiful to see! God made you an incredible man, and made you to support a wife with a passion to free others to do what they were called to do. When questioned by anyone, know when to "shake the dust off your feet" (Matthew 10:14) say, "God bless and thanks for your thoughts," and turn your caring eyes toward Jesus, the Healer. Continue to do exactly what you are doing. Ask for prayer, share your thoughts, and let's get Shelley healed and back to fighting the GOOD fight! Amen? Don't ever feel like you need to justify your good and decent and Christ centered actions to anyone. You've got Shelley's back, and we've got yours. God's blessings, Dr. B

I also knew something else was happening on this ICU floor that I was not fully understanding yet. More and more doctors were stopping in, for no more reason than to look at Shelley. More medical personnel were present at her door during rounds than any other patient. There were hushed conversations, lots of fretting over scans and test results, and a never-ending stream of doctors and nurses coming in, asking her name and if she could make a thumbs up with her right hand, and leaving with a shocked look.

All these things seemed positive, but I was also struggling with some real fear. Shelley didn't understand why she was in the hospital, at one point telling one of the doctors she was there for a broken back, but not to tell Tim (me), because I would be really sad. All the tubes and catheters were becoming bothersome, and it was a constant struggle to keep her from ripping things out of her body. Shelley was also hallucinating, seeing people and animals that were not in the room. At one point, I had to pretend to remove a snake she saw from the bed to calm her down. She offered all her doctors and nurses to join her for a glass of wine on the second floor, and asked me to put a brisket in the oven to feed all the guests that were coming over. Sometimes she knew she was in the hospital and wanted to leave, other times she thought we were home and wanted me to let the dogs in. All of this and her voice was a scratchy whisper at best, making her hard to understand and frustrating her with the lack of the ability to communicate.

There were also moments of complete lucidity. It was like her brain was fighting through the cloudiness to reach out to me. At one point, Shelley reached with her hand to pull my head to hers. She pushed our foreheads together and said, "Don't worry, I'm strong, we will be okay. You are my person."

That last sentence was something Shelley said to me a lot at night while going to bed. It was her love language for me. Hearing her say that gave me a lot of relief, and then a minute later she was talking to one of the machines next to her bed like it was a live human.

I texted Shelley's phone before trying to go to sleep for a couple hours that night.

Trying to get you to go to sleep now that you are awake is a real challenge. But on the positive side you told me I'm your person. So, I'll take it! Love you so much.

Monday, April 17th – Let's Get Out of Here

Day 13 - It must be frustrating for her. Every single person that walks in the room asks her what her name is, can she wiggle her toes, does she know where she is…every time she answers correctly it's a victory, but sometimes she won't or can't answer and for her that is discouraging. I try to stay focused on the positive and relish the moments that are near normal as glimpses of hope for the future.

ICU delirium. Look it up. There are times it's scarier than anything else we've overcome so far. Coupled with the difficulties created by a hemorrhagic brain injury, it has made today very challenging.

I just keep praying for her numbers to improve, for her medication levels to keep dropping, and for her mind to be at peace with where she is and what goals are set out ahead of her. Tonight, we need rest and regular old-fashioned sleep. Thank you to everyone again for your support. Tomorrow will be two weeks in the ICU. Hoping we have a solid day of progress.

That is all I have for today. I'm feeling a little more tired than usual. Hopefully I can get some decent sleep tonight too.

• • • •

I CAN'T EVEN BEGIN to describe the nightmare that is ICU delirium. This was the hardest day yet. The hallucinations were getting worse. Shelley's eyes dart around thinking she sees people that are not there. She has lost track of time and why she is even in the hospital. It was even more problematic because as her body regained strength, she was constantly trying to sit up, get out of bed, and mess with all the tubes and wires attached to her. There was real danger of her pulling out an arterial line, her EVD, or central catheter. Her emotions were in a constant state of flux, and she had become fixated on things outside her control to the point of anger. For example, she was off the charts mad that she isn't allowed to get out of bed to urinate; so mad, she was adamant I do not leave the room to go the bathroom because it was the one thing she wanted to do and couldn't. Another conversation went something like this.

Shelley: "Babe, get my stuff, and let's get out of here."

Me: (exasperated because this is the tenth time we have had this conversation) - "I'm sorry, we can't."

Shelley: "No... babe... go get the car and I'll meet you downstairs."

Me: "Honey, we can't go."

Shelley: "WHHHYYYY?"

Me: "Well, for starters, you have a drain hose coming out of your brain attached to that bag of fluid hanging over there. It is extremely dangerous for you to go anywhere right now."

Shelley: "So?"

Me: "And we can't take all this machinery and medicine with us. You are hooked up to too many things."

Shelley: "Well, just unplug them."

Me: " You will die."

Shelley: (rolls her eyes and starts sliding her leg off the bed)

Me: Please, stop, or they will have to restrain you.

Shelley: (stops and closes eyes for a couple minutes then suddenly says) - "Babe, why aren't you driving?"

We look back on it now and have a little chuckle; but at the time, it was downright scary and frustrating for everyone. All of us wanted to do anything we could to make her comfortable, help her understand the situation, and hasten recovery as quickly as possible; however, all we were doing was making her salty.

Shelley's daughter had brought a stuffed bear that you could warm up in a microwave and put some lavender oil on to help calm her.

Somehow, it became a real person to Shelley, one that she didn't want in the room. The bear went from her bed to the couch, to the window sill, and finally down to the waiting room.

I am telling you ICU delirium is REAL.

Shelley was worried about a man in the corner who was watching her, and at times she would direct me where to stand in the room to block his view. Of course, there was no man there, but I complied, hoping it would make her feel better.

The TV monitor attached to the specialized blood pressure monitor next to her bed was a target of extended conversation from Shelley. It never spoke back, at least not that I heard, but Shelley was carrying on an entire conversation with it, even arguing over something at one point.

One of the nurses explained to me that Shelley needed sleep. Being in a coma apparently wasn't "good sleep," and she was delirious from lack of rest. We had spent all this prayer time waking her up. Maybe we had prayed too hard for that! Now we needed to pray for her to sleep!

One positive sign was that she now recognized everyone that came into the room. While she sometimes struggled with names, you could see the recognition on her face, and the fact that she knew all her family was reassuring. I was allowing a few close friends in to see her, hoping it would help distract her and raise her spirits.

Our home church, King's Trail Cowboy Church, was really fired up in prayer. The amount of energy coming from the pastors, worship team, staff, and congregation was so powerful that at times I felt guilty. We did not deserve that kind of attention; however, they wouldn't have it any other way. Our pastor, Jason, regularly brought me a sandwich and we would eat together and discuss everything going on. His prayers in Shelley's room were especially powerful.

The Prayer Chain for Shelley Luther Facebook group was also filled with prayers, more than a person could count daily. There was another one that caught my attention when I read them that night.

Dear Lord, I'm so grateful that we can come to You at any time and from anywhere and lift up Shelley, Tim, and their Families to You. Thank You that You hear our prayers and answer them according to Your perfect will. Lord, I pray, considering all the logistical things that need to take place on a daily basis when meeting Shelley's needs while in the hospital, I pray, God, that You would ensure she is handled with the utmost care, honor, respect, and dignity. Lord, I pray the hospital staff would be tenderhearted, gentle, and respectful as they help care for her daily needs. Please help Shelley to trust and understand they are there to help and care for her and that she would NOT feel stressed, uncomfortable...or the need to wrestle with anyone. Thank You that Tim and others are standing watch to advocate for Shelley. And that YOU are their Advocate! I also pray You would provide at least one healthcare worker who is also a Christian; someone who could provide an even deeper level of care to Shelley, Tim, and their Family, through the power of Your Holy Spirit. Lord, we thank You for all You're going to do today. We speak LIFE, HEALING, STRENGTH and WHOLENESS over Shelley, in Jesus' Name. We speak ENERGY, STRENGTH, and ENCOURAGEMENT over Tim, in Jesus' Name. And we ask You to fill them both with courage, resilience, and determination, in Jesus' Name.

What was interesting about this prayer was the ask for a Christian healthcare worker. Ever since Shelley had woken up, we had a lot of healthcare workers in and out of the room. Many of them asked about the prayer shawl that had been laying across her legs nearly every hour of every day. Some touched it before leaving the room to go to their next destination. I even had seen nurses come in during the middle of the night to touch it before hurrying back to their own patients' rooms. I had no way of knowing if all these people were Christians, but whatever they believed, they were being drawn to the amount of prayer that was being directed into our room.

Another church, The Branch, where we assisted with leading worship, had also been throwing up a huge amount of prayer. One of their worship team members contacted me to let me know they had stopped mid-service one evening to ask God to intervene for Shelley. Their pastor, Chris, had been communicating with me as well, and sharing prayer and positive thoughts with me.

The number of messages, prayers, and advice I was receiving daily was staggering. Some people were asking if I was singing to her, or if I was playing worship music for her. I wasn't. Not because I didn't want to, but because contrary to what people liked to think about us, we didn't spend all our free time making or listening to music. That was our job, and it was done in a very focused manner. If we were listening to or making music, it was either serious rehearsal or serious performance. We gave our minds and ears breaks from the noise when we could. This did make me think about it a bit, and I tried to play some worship music for her to help relax her, and it only seemed to agitate and stir her up.

Another friend sent me a testimony about their experience with ICU delirium.

Tim, I would like to share something with you if I may. My mom was real sick last Christmas. We thought we were going to lose her they could never really figure out what caused the issues. She passed out kind foamed out of her mouth her bodily functions let loose .my dad thought she was dying. She had a seizure . She was rushed to the hospital by ambulance . They kept her there did a bunch of test weren't real what was going on . They released her to go home she was not doing better and ambulance took her back to the hospital they kind of tossed diagnoses around like that broken heart syndrome because her best friend died her sister died my brother got a DUI stress of Christmas so that broken heart syndrome can cause an adrenaline to your heart and make your heart beat irregular they weren't even real sure about that but the point I wanted to share was with you is ICU psychosis and delirium is a very real thing. My mom did not recognize my dad and I... she said some real crazy things was completely out of her head. She wasn't there at all. She didn't understand she couldn't answer those questions that Shelley's being asked sometimes she would sometimes she wouldn't we didn't know what we were dealing with either. My parents have been married 57 years ... they wanted us to take to my mom to a "rehab place" but attached to rehab was nursing home. My dad said absolutely not he said I just want to get your mom home. I agreed we were going to do whatever was needed to do if that was our new norm. I had considered moving in with them going to work from there we had talked it out my dad and I made a commitment to each other that we weren't going to put her in a rehab we were going to take her home and take our chances. It was extremely hard in the beginning because that delirium and psychosis doesn't go away as quick as you get home. Mom was very confused she was scared she didn't feel like her home was her home, she thought it was all backwards Her mind was not in a good place when we brought her home there was glimpses of normal but a lot of abnormal. We kept validating her answering her questions honestly repeating repetitive questions we continue to assure her as best as we could her life. She would get up in the middle of the night and roam the house at night move things around talking in her sleep say crazy stuff it was a slow process and took several months but she came around. That's the message I want you to receive is she did come around and she's back to herself 100%. She didn't know what happened in the hospital, still ask a lot of questions and sometimes gets confused but I have my mom back and my dad has his wife back. So, I want you to gain from this is it can be done with patience and love and understanding honesty reassurance they can come back to you 100%. It wasn't an easy road, but it was the path we were insistent upon taking and luckily, we did because if we would've put her in a home, we would've never got her back. So, you're not alone although it seems very scary and it's very hurtful when she looks at you like a stranger, I know that deep pain because my mom didn't recognize my face... Just don't give up and you can beat that nasty disease of ICU psychosis and dementia. Sorry if this messages all over the place, I'm doing it as I'm crying because it brought back so many memories, but I felt the need to share it with you .

If you need someone to talk to who is experienced it I'm here for you I know we were kind of just superficial friends but I lived your nightmare and I know all too well what you're going through. Also, a piece of advice is to take care of your health as well. I had to force my dad to walk away when my mom was screaming at him because she was so angry when he wouldn't take her home... We had to walk away from the hospital and put trust in the hospital that they would care for her when moments got too tough for us because of the things she would say to us the pain would hurt so deeply and it wasn't her talking to us... so take care of yourself because she needs you to be 100% ... I didn't do that very well so that's why I am telling you to selfishly take a second or hour for yourself... you have to be good to help her... good luck... I am here if you have questions. I will be praying for you.

Someone who lived not too far from us sent me another testimony.

Traumatic brain injuries are hard on a spouse just as much as the patient. My husband was in a motorcycle accident while we were dating, no helmet, he was in a coma for two weeks. He was in ICU for a month rehab for a month and I'm a nurse so I would take care of him when he got home. He went through bouts of gratefulness, anger, all kinds of things, he was grateful we got married not long after that it turned to anger and he goes through really bad bouts of anger so it's hard for a spouse. Also, TBI's are not easy to handle. We've been praying for her, and I've been praying for both of you because I know how it's gonna look on your end because I live it every day. I hope she fully recovers. It's a long road and we are six years into this road. He died twice before he was even care flighted did, he died again at the hospital but he's living but he does not have a lot of memory, short-term memory, long-term memory. He's a retired canine cop, and he doesn't even remember half of his career. He's fully functioning at work, but the anger part and the loss of patience is hard. We have been together praying for you guys. Just want you to know.

It was so much. I was so tired. Shelley was so frustrated, angry, and scared. My text to her phone that night reflected all that.

Tonight has been the most difficult night yet. It's so painful to see you struggle so hard and be so scared. One minute I think you are calm, the next you are so angry that I won't take you home. I want to take you home honey, so bad, we just can't go yet. I love you; I am so sorry this is happening to you.

While I laid there on the couch in her room, amidst the beeps, whistles, and symphony of sounds that is the ICU, I couldn't help but ask, "God, why are You doing this to me? How do I support and protect my wife from things that are not real?"

God hears our prayers, and sometimes he answers instantly. This time he answered through Shelley's voice.

"Hey babe," Shelley called out to me, and I leaned over from the chair next to her bed so she could speak directly to me.

"I know the things I am seeing aren't real, like they really are not there. But they feel real. They feel real to me even though they aren't really there, and I need you to understand that. I hear you when you say they aren't there, but that doesn't help make the feeling go away. So can you just help me with it when it happens?"

I nodded my head yes, took her hand, and together we spent the night fighting her hallucinations like we did everything in our life, together.

Day 14 - I am feeling pretty wiped out today and wasn't really able to put into words where we were today, then I saw my sister-in-law, Keri Shea Byrd's post, and feel like she said it best. So, I'm copying and pasting from her tonight.

. . . .

(KERI) THANK YOU ALL for the continued prayers!! THEY ARE WORKING!! This picture is perfect showing the POWER my sister can display, and the effort she is currently trying to get her strength/mind/body back.

Her spirit NEVER left! Shelley has been removed off the ventilator and breathing on her own and trying desperately to speak and share her love for family and support. Her mind gets a little jumbled at times, but that is to be expected with hemorrhaging brain injury and 10 days in a coma. Her vitals and cranial pressures are still a little wacky with her brain drain still inserted and helping relieve excess pressure, and we are still in the 'danger zone' for another stroke and seizures. My prayer request is that she is rid of the major anxiety due to ICU delirium causing scary hallucinations. As her brain creates new pathways and tries to restore her beautiful, creative mind. Yall, she is fighting so hard. She is trapped in a mind that has suffered much trauma, but she WILL fight. I also ask for prayers for her husband Tim. He has been a BOULDER of a rock and has stood by her side every second. He has to witness the love of his life scared to death while fighting with every bit of energy she has to get well 24 hours a day. I pray he gets rest to be restored daily. At times there are moments of joy... she told me she loved me, she mumbled she is aware of her ruptured brain aneurysm, and she said the nurses and doctors are 'phenomenal'! We have been given some upsetting news about health coverage and given an estimate of what the current bill is to date, and I am praying on how to help Tim handle that. So many of you have asked how you can help, offered food, rides, airline miles for our family, help with her rescue ranch, and 24-hour prayer chains and so on and so on. THANK YOU!!! The support has restored my thoughts on humanity and just how beautiful God's children are when we come together after being witness to someone they care for unexpectedly is fighting for precious life and their family in desperate pain. Shelley has a message to spread of Gods miracle of how the doctors, nurses and support have helped us reach this far. She is just the voice to do it. We just need her to stay calm and rest so we can get her to the next phase of physical/mental recovery. My family thanks all of you from a place in our hearts that can only be expressed by unconditional love. Thank you...thank you thank you. Shelley needs us all to BELIEVE she can beat this and stand and walk out of that hospital bed that she was once imprisoned to on life support. I have a completely different perspective on life, and I won't let a day go by without telling those I love just how much they mean to me. So, thank you all. KEEP BELIEVING!

I am glad Keri had the energy and optimism for that post because I didn't. I am not sure if I had slept at all the night before. Shelley tried to get up no less than two dozen times throughout the night, and finally wore herself out as the sun was coming up. I sent this text to our family.

We had a pretty rough night. She slept from about 1am-3am, but spent most of the rest of the night unable to relax enough to sleep. She said she knows the things she keeps seeing are not real, but they feel real and that scares her. I spent most of the night holding her hand and trying to comfort her as well as keep her from trying to get up out of bed several times. She finally just fell asleep

again around 7am, and they are going to let her sleep for a while even though it's morning.

I let her daughter, Rachael, and father look after her during the late morning so I could go grab a shower and a quick nap at my dad's house. When I returned to the hospital and entered Shelley's room, they were in the middle of collecting urine for a test. Maybe it was coincidence, or maybe it was my wife seeing me come back, but her blood pressure instantly spiked and there was a scramble to see what was going on. In the middle of the chaos, I kicked over the urine cup, and basically just made a mess out of everything.

It was embarrassing, and after apologizing to the nurses and making sure her blood pressure was okay, I walked back down to the waiting room. My dad's wife Carol was in there writing in a journal book that Rachael had been keeping for her mom.

Shelley, our phone rang very early on a Wednesday morning and I held my breath hoping it wasn't bad news. We spent the next two weeks trying to convince our Lord to let us keep you for a little while longer. So many prayers. Now we give thanks, but I don't know how we can ever give enough thanks for this miracle. I will be working on that question for a very long time. Love Always, Carol

Miracle, sometimes I think people overuse that word. The official definition in the Oxford dictionary is a surprising and welcome event that is not explicable by natural or scientific laws and is therefore considered to be the work of a divine agency. This instance was not an overuse of the word miracle. In fact, maybe the word miracle wasn't representative enough of what we were going through. The end of the definition bothered me, though. The work of a divine agency? What is wrong with saying God?

Shelley had suffered a ruptured brain aneurysm that killed most people before they ever even made it to the hospital, and she endured transfer to a different hospital and a failed surgery. Her odds of survival were so small they hardly registered a number. Then she had suffered no fewer than half a dozen strokes that were supposed to cripple her right side and prevent her from talking, yet there she was moving her entire body and talking with everyone in the room. We still had a long way to go, but there was no other explanation than God had intervened. Thousands upon thousands of people were praying.

Something was really tugging at my subconscious about all of this. What was God expecting from us? My mind was too tired to try and make sense of any of it. I think it was that fatigue that allowed my mind to be open to God's suggestion. I was not trying to overthink it, and God gave me a word.

"Share."

My first thought was how I was already sharing, and as He often does, God clarified his word for me.

"More."

It was then I started taking a lot more copious notes. Apparently, Facebook wasn't going to be enough.

Day 15 - Half a month in the ICU. Hard to believe. I couldn't tell you if time has gone by fast or slow, it's just happening. One thing that I think a lot of people say that has become a little cliche in our language is "don't take anything for granted," and the intention is to remember not to waste a day not doing something or loving someone with your whole heart. I totally agree with that sentiment, but watching Shelley battle in the ICU brings "taking something for granted" to a whole new level. Be thankful you can breathe without a machine helping you; that you can swallow without danger of asphyxiation, or even swallow at all for that matter; that you can chew food; that you can get up out of bed. These seemingly simple and sometimes automated body processes should not be taken for granted. There is a whole floor of patients here learning how to sip and swallow water, and may go for weeks without any type of food or drink in their mouth. The discouragement that accompanies attempting these tasks is painful, both for the patient and the family.

Last night was really hard. As Shelley continues to become more aware of what's happened and going on around her, she also has moments where she just wants to go home so badly that it is really upsetting to her. We've prayed so hard for her to wake up, and now it seems like we need to pray for her to get real sleep. Every time she does, she comes back more lucid and stronger than ever. When she tires out, the ICU delirium kicks in. Her strength is best suited for the battlefield, not the hospital bed, and it's that challenge we are trying hardest to overcome.

Today has been the best day so far, and the doctors feel like she is improving steadily. Some vital numbers are still off, but clinically she is doing well, so rather than chase numbers, we are just continuing to push ahead and let her body heal without trying more surgeries. Today was the last day of the first danger window where they watch for potential vasospasms in her brain. If we can get past that window of danger then we can start looking at taking the vent out of her skull.

A lot of people have been asking about our upcoming show schedule. All our future Crush events are currently cancelled or on hold. We don't have any idea what the future holds for that right now. I am keeping several of my upcoming solo and dueling commitments on the schedule that are local; I'll post about them as I make my decisions. A lot of it will have to do with how Shelley's recovery is coming and how comfortable I am being away from the hospital.

I want to especially thank Kyle and Mark for their help and support in getting some financial assistance to help see us through the time off, medical bills, therapy, and recovery time that will be coming up. So many of you have chipped in and been so supportive. I can't tell you how much we appreciate it. We are slowly starting to accept some visitors, just be patient and understand Shelley is still in an ICU. If you think you'd like to stop by, contact me, and depending on how the day is going I know she would love to say hi.

* * * *

THIS WAS A BIG DAY for us in a lot of ways. Shelley asked for her phone, attempted to make some calls, but was struggling to use her fingers to touch the screen correctly to dial. She was being a little stubborn about it, but finally let me help her dial, and she started calling family that wasn't there at the hospital. She also attempted to read some texts and messages; however, I soon realized her brain had not worked reading and comprehension out yet.

They did a swallow test to see if they could remove the feeding tube and allow her to begin eating real food, but she did not pass it, meaning she was still going to have to be content on sucking on ice chips and being allowed the tiniest bit of applesauce to practice swallowing.

There had been a code blue two rooms down the hall from us in the middle of the night, and Shelley had asked me what was going on. When I explained to her that someone had been having a severe medical emergency, and later they had passed, she cried not knowing who the person even was. I did not tell her we had met all their family in the waiting room and shared our Easter dinner with them. I figured it would be too much for her.

Her dad had left to go home that morning, her sister was due back in another day or two, as was her mom. For a couple days it was just going to be me, her two daughters, and my dad and his wife. The shift was rotating. It also meant I had to keep everyone a little better informed via text.

So, the night was pretty tough again. As she gets stronger and able to move more, she has become more belligerent about staying in bed and leaving her wires and tubes alone. We have had a 24-hour sitter in the room, but today they told me if a family member isn't in the room at all times, they will need to restrain her arms. Her hallucinations are still pretty vivid. On the plus side her memory and acceptance of where she is and what is going on continues to improve. Of course, she decided it's nap time right now as every doctor is about to show up.

The word belligerent probably wasn't strong enough. The previous night had been a huge debacle. Shelley was constantly picking at the oxygen monitor taped to her finger, tugging at her feeding tube, and messing with her arterial line. The nurse had finally put some mittens on her that were supposed to keep her from being able to grab anything. They also had tethers on them if she continued to mess with things and they needed to tie her down.

This was a huge source of discomfort and consternation for Shelley. She argued with the patient observer in her room about it for about thirty minutes before giving up and going to sleep; or should I say pretending to go to sleep?

After it appeared that Shelley was in a deep sleep, the patient observer told me she was going to slip out to the restroom and grab a quick snack. I assured her I had everything under control. She hadn't been gone for more than ten seconds when Shelley started crying and sobbing to me.

"Babe, please take these gloves off my hands. They are killing me. I can't explain what it feels like, but I just need them off. Please."

"No, honey, they are for your own protection right now. Please, don't get so upset, just try to relax," I told her. There was no amount of begging that was going to get me to take those mittens off her hands.

"Why are you doing this to me? You don't understand how I feel," she was at a full cry now. "Why do you hate me? Why are you making me wear these? I won't do anything bad."

This conversation went on for a couple more minutes. Watching my wife cry after being in the hospital for over two weeks was too much. I finally relented and agreed to take one mitten off if she promised not to mess with anything. I removed the mitten from her right hand and turned to place it on the counter. My back was turned for less than five seconds. When I turned back around, Shelley had pulled her feeding tube completely out and was looking at the end of it dripping onto her bedsheet. She had also managed to rip the oxygen sensor off her fingertip and the monitor started beeping, alerting the nurse to come in.

"I only turned my back for a couple of seconds," I stammered.

"How did she get her glove off?"

Needless to say, I got a good scolding from the nurses and attendant. Because Shelley had not had any type of nutrition while ventilated, and only from the feeding tube the last couple days, it needed to be put back in right away, and in the middle of the night which took up a lot of valuable staff time.

At least Shelley seemed sorry, if not a little amused that she had fooled all of us. She was not amused when the nurses demanded me restrain her arms as she fought the replacement of the tube.

"I'm going to count to ten," she told me while I held her arm down.

"And then what," I responded, completely exasperated and exhausted.

"And then I'm leaving. One, two, three..."

I actually laughed, which only infuriated her. The nurses could see the situation was worsening quickly, and one of them took over for me and told me to go to the waiting room. I went down to the "apartment" and pulled a bag of chips out of one of the goody baskets and a cold Dr. Pepper out of the cooler. My wife was back, but not in the way I had hoped for. Even though she was awake, she wasn't the life partner that I relied on, at least not yet.

In the stack of snacks, drinks, and get-well gifts, someone had left a bible. It was brand new; I could tell it had probably only been opened a couple times. Our pastor spends a lot of time teaching about how everything we need we can find in the Word, so I picked the bible up and let it fall open. I was in the book of Philippians, and it only took me a few verses to stumble onto Philippians 4:6; "Do not be anxious about anything, but in every situation, by prayer and petition, with thanksgiving, present your requests to God."

"What do you think I've been doing?" I think I said it out loud, angry with myself, angry with the entire situation really.

I closed the bible and let it fall open again. Eventually my eyes landed on John 13:7; "Jesus replied, 'You do not realize now what I am doing, but later you will understand.'"

The Word was definitely right about that! I didn't understand anything right now. I sat and ate my snack in silence, thinking about what I had read. When I finished, I walked back through the ICU toward Shelley's room. Through every door was a patient that was in some sort of imminent trouble. Most still had ventilators. Some were restrained. Some had no family or friends staying with them, just lying by themselves in the glow of the computer monitors over their beds. Some had EVD vents in their skulls, some had tracheostomy tubes in their throats, and others had complete portions of their skulls removed. One of the rooms looked like a bomb had gone off in it. The patient had broken out of his restraints and pulled a computer monitor off the wall, tipped over the IV stands and poles holding his medications, and tried to run down the hall while in the process of losing his hospital gown. He had been moved somewhere else. One of the patients who had stepped down out of the ICU a couple days ago was back, their condition deteriorating rapidly outside of the critical care received in the specialty unit. Several of the rooms were empty, and I knew those patients had not been in good enough condition to leave the ICU unless it was with a sheet over their body.

"God, I am thankful I haven't had to endure that," I prayed to myself as I entered Shelley's room. She was asleep, and I sat down on the couch. Maybe that's what I needed to learn tonight. To be patient, God had everything under control, and to be thankful for the progress that Shelley had made so far. It was past midnight and when I checked Facebook, a memory from three years ago was staring me in the face. April 20th, 2020 was the day Shelley had announced we were going to reopen the salon against the Covid ordinances that had shut down "non-essential" businesses. Shelley had always told me that God had given her the courage to do that, and had promised He would protect her.

Maybe my life partner was helping me more than I thought, even when she seemed incapable.

"God, thank you for giving me back my wife. Please give me the same courage she showed three years ago. Help me to be patient and have faith that You have everything under control. Finally, continue to give us hope and let us take a couple small steps forward tomorrow."

I finished praying and I heard my wife stir.

"Babe," she whispered, turning her head away from the observer that was sitting on the other side of the bed, "Get my things and let's get out of here."

Thursday, April 20th – Two Little Steps

Day 16 - Three years ago today, Shelley announced we were reopening the salon. That decision sent us on one of the wildest rides I ever could have imagined. I never saw a person with as much courage and conviction as she had during that time. Fast forward three years and I understand the frustration she feels when sitting up on the side of the bed, being helped to take two steps before having to lay back down again. But the miracle is that she actually took steps! A week ago, the doctors were warning us of possible paralysis in the right side of her body. She continues to fight her way back, and for those of us on the outside it is thrilling and a huge sense of relief. For her, it's another battle that she is refusing to lose, and I'm so proud of how hard she is trying.

Her EVD (external ventricular drain) is clamped tonight, meaning for the first time in 16 days we get to see if her cranial cavity is going to maintain the correct pressure. This is frightening for me, as it is the primary indicator of whether or not her brain is in danger of more damage. A successful night will be a huge step forward and 24 hours closer to possibly removing the vent. I am praying that prayer for her tonight, because I want her to feel that sense of victory and progress that she is trying so hard to achieve.

The nights are still hard. Insomnia, hallucinations, the ICU delirium. We have to have a sitter in the room, even with me there. Even if you finally can get her to relax, a code blue on the floor, a 3am CT scan, or the hourly wellness check reawakens her and the process of trying to settle back into sleep starts all over again. The quicker we can get stepped down from ICU, the better.

We have had several people making extraordinary efforts to help. I'm going to try and link their projects in the comments

below. As always, we are thankful for everyone who has prayed for us. We are blessed to have such amazing family and friends.

• • • •

SOMETIMES I THINK GOD likes to show us that not only is He listening, but He is going to answer with a little sense of humor. Shelley had a visit from a physical therapist today, and much to our surprise, she sat Shelley up on the side of the bed, had her stand up, take one step to the side, and then lay back down. I had prayed to God the night before for a couple small steps forward. His answer was a couple steps to the side. Ok Lord, you have my attention.

It sounds simple, but after being in bed for sixteen days, losing twenty pounds, being in a coma, and having too many surgeries to count, taking two steps was a huge deal. I could tell Shelley felt both victorious and frustrated at the same time, but we were experiencing other little victories that definitely were giving all of us hope. Her bad fever had finally subsided, and they were able to remove the central catheter and machine that cooled her blood. Watching them pull the ten-inch spike out of her groin made me woozy. Not only was this a lot of physical relief for her, but the machinery noise in the room was also reduced dramatically.

It had been sixteen days since she had brushed her teeth, and she really wanted to do that, but she was on so much blood thinner, the doctors did not want to risk a gum bleed. Her hair had not been washed or brushed in sixteen days either, but with the EVD in her skull, that was going to have to wait as well.

I was amazed at some of the things being done by people for Shelley. Candida Hernandez-Carter was hand drawing a beautiful picture of Shelley singing to auction off at a benefit concert being held for Shelley. She was also making multiple prints for us. Blessed Mess Boutique was making a "Pray for Shelley" T-shirt with a picture of

Shelley on it. When I shared these things with Shelley, she would tear up and ask me why they would do that for her.

I thought back to 2020, after the Texas Supreme Court had released her from jail, we had been blessed with a lot of donations to help with the legal fees. After paying the legal fees, there was still quite a bit left, in fact it would have been enough to pay off our home mortgage, buy several new cars, or spend in any multitude of ways. Instead, she put the money into a charity and gave it all away. We left a $1,000 tip to a waitress working at a nearly empty restaurant who had to leave her apartment and move in with her daughter. We gave $18,000 to a homeless man who was trying to finish barber school to help pay his tuition and get him a place to live. We hired a friend to repaint our home, only because he refused to accept a gift from us. Shelley had always given everything she had to everyone else, so the answer to her question was simple. People were doing things for her because she spent her life doing things for everyone else. Comments on my Facebook post also reinforced what I was trying to tell her.

From Lettie:

Three years ago today she became our super hero. One day I'll share that story. She is brave as heck and above that she is kind and compassionate. I will never forget what she did for me. I pray for her and you everyday. One day we will all celebrate and share stories. Stories of love and faith.

From PJ:

Taking steps!!!! Tim, this is a post so many of us rejoice reading! Yes, they're small and they're assisted but SHELLEY is taking them!

This woman made an impression on thousands of us three years ago on THIS DAY - standing against an overreaching government. Today, she is standing again - tired but determined and unwilling to give up. So proud of her and so thankful to God for answered prayers.

Tonight will be another huge milestone - and we're claiming that blessing right now.

Dear Lord, we ask you to give Shelley and Tim much needed rest and sleep tonight. We praise you for her progress this far and we know you're holding her and giving her the strength to keep fighting.

Amen.

I also ran across a comment that made me smile from Fran:

For the past 24 hours a song I heard you and Shelley sing once has been going through my head. I don't know the name, but the chorus goes boom, boom, boom, boom, boom, boom, boom ,boom, boom! I suppose the past two weeks have been a serious boom to your lives. But as I hear the song in my head, I imagine the next booms will be progress. Boom! She's awake. Boom! She's speaking. Boom! She's walking. I'm praying for the big Boom when she gets to go home and you guys get to resume your lives. Love you both!

This gave me a good chuckle. The song Fran was referring to was "Super Bass" by Nicki Minaj. Shelley did a great job performing this song, and it always surprised a lot of people when we would do it, either with our band, or just the two of us. The song always packed the dance floor when we performed it, but I really liked it because of a few of the lyrics in it. The "boom" Fran was referring to was the singer's heartbeat – "Boy, you got my heartbeat runnin' away, don't you hear that heartbeat coming your way? Oh, it be like boom, badoom…"

Music can mean so many different things to so many people, and Shelley touched so many hearts from the stage and the worship platform. Sharing that space with her was one of the most intimate moments a couple can have with one another. While everyone was dancing on the dance floor, my wife and I were having a "conversation" with each other on stage. In the aforementioned song, she is telling me how her heart beats for me. I missed that connection with my wife. It had been over two weeks since we had made music together, and I realized I was dreading tomorrow. I had to do my first show since her aneurysm had burst, and I had to do it without her.

Friday, April 21ˢᵗ – My Sky Full of Stars

Day 17 - Another day of little steps forward. We keep getting good news and more tubes are coming off. It's bittersweet, because Shelley was supposed to be on this show with me tonight. I'm grateful that our family is there for her this evening while I play, and I'm honored to have my good friend and dueling mentor Tom with me tonight.

Tonight I'm praying for Shelley to remain focused on her goals, not to be discouraged by the length of the road ahead, and for her continued healing.

And finally, honey, I'll be back soon. This one's for you.

• • • •

"I JUST SHUT I A SHINY Shemane"

That was the first text sent by Shelley since April 4ᵗʰ. None of us know for sure what it meant. She had her phone sitting by her hospital bed to talk with family that wasn't at the hospital. It would be several days before she attempted to send a text again, but the combination of shaky inaccurate fingers and a brain that wasn't reading letters clearly were the main culprits for this cryptic message. She did send this message after her first visit to the portable toilet they brought near her bed that day. I will leave it to the reader to try and translate what she meant.

Most of the day was spent doing little tests and exercises to see what parts of her body were working, what needed exercise, and what needed more rest. Her urinary catheter was able to be removed, and she was allowed to sit up and move to a hospital chair or the portable toilet in the room with help and observation of the nurses. There was also a plethora of tests that involved trying to swallow, blowing into different types of tubes to measure her lung strength, and of course being taken for CT scans to watch her brain ventricles to see if they were draining properly. The doctors were talking about getting the EVD out of her head, and her cranial pressure had been staying stable for the past twenty-four hours.

Therapists of all sorts were stopping in to exercise her legs, her arms, and check her neurological progress. While it was exciting for us to see her making so much progress, it was frustrating at times for Shelley. Part of her understood what had happened and the long road ahead, and part of her just wanted to leave the hospital and didn't comprehend the hold up.

The biggest struggle for me, though, was going to perform a show that night. Shelley and I did almost all our work together. It was one of the blessings we shared with each other, to be able to work together doing something we loved. I felt guilty for leaving the hospital, and guilty for performing without her.

Driving to the theater that evening reminded me of the solo shows and other gigs I used to do before Shelley and I got married and committed ourselves to working together as much as possible. When I had first started dating Shelley, she would come see some of my solo shows, and I had my own arrangement of a song titled Sky Full of Stars by Coldplay that I would do. In my mind, the lyrics of the song were for her, and I never really knew if she noticed them or not. Sometimes I thought I would catch her listening, other times she would be talking with friends, and I assumed it was something she was not catching on to.

I quit doing that song once we were performing together, but was caught off guard one night when she turned to me on stage and said, "Play that song you always used to sing to me about the sky full of stars."

She had been listening.

I think that is one of the things that is special about my wife. Even when you think she isn't paying attention, she hears and files that memory away.

The show went great, and the theater was filled with people who wanted to know how Shelley was doing. Tom and I took requests and played for nearly two hours straight. Several of the request slips that came up were asking for songs for Shelley as well as asking for a current update. Near the end of the evening, I told them that story and played my arrangement of Sky Full of Stars. I could barely keep myself together enough to make it through the song, but I managed to do it. One of the lines of the song really stood out to me differently than it had before.

"Cause you get lighter the more it gets dark..." Shelley is definitely like that. She shines when it's darkest and times are toughest. So does Jesus.

My dueling piano partner that night was Tom Basler, a dueling veteran, trainer, and mentor that had taken me under his wing when I was new to the dueling scene. Shelley and I both really enjoyed our times performing with Tom, and he has always been a good friend, an honest partner, and now a brother in Christ. Tom and I had some time to talk about how things were going, and he shared with me how his spiritual journey had been going, and that seeing me, and Shelley go through this trial had only strengthened his desire to continue to grow stronger in his faith. I had goosebumps leaving the theater that night, like God was telling me, "See, look what sharing this experience with others can do?"

The drive back to the hospital could not have seemed slower. I wanted to get back to my wife as quickly as possible, but Keri's flight had been delayed and she was now stuck at the airport. The rental car agencies were either closed or sold out of cars and she needed a ride. This gave me a lot of time to think about that line from the song. Undoubtedly, I was in one of the toughest situations in my life, and the spiritual fire was burning brighter than ever to help guide me. I just needed to stay obedient and focused. Every time I had doubts, every time the road seemed dark ahead; I just needed to have faith, and apparently a whole lot of prayer!

I couldn't believe the number of people that were praying for her, and for us. Nearly every person exiting the theater that night had stopped to tell me they were praying for us. My phone and social media were full of positive messages. The prayer chains, the churches, it was all so overwhelming – in a good way. But it was also making me start to think that this was another lesson God wanted me to learn.

I had always been a bit cynical about "thoughts and prayers." I felt like it was an easy thing to say, and I always wanted to know what the prayer was, or what action was being taken with the prayer. But now, God was showing me when people said they were praying, they really were praying. People were sending me prayers, thousands of them. When I arrived at the airport, I had a few minutes to wait while Keri's shuttle arrived, and I read some of the prayers from the prayer chain page and messenger on Facebook.

Thank you for sharing!!! Beautiful talent. I continue to pray for Shelley. There is no greater power than that of our Savior. He knows Shelley by name. He is the creator of her strength, her chutzpah, and her passionate purpose yet to fulfill.

Tim and Shelley: I will stand in agreement before The Throne on your behalf...I just read your update and am so excited to see Him working....even if it's not "fast enough" for our human minds...

He Is Working....I hope to be able to hug you in person very soon.

I know you don't know me, but we go to church together, and I have been praying for Shelley. ICU delirium is real and so tough. You are doing great. I am a night shift ICU RN, and I just want to tell you to try to rest too. You are doing great for her, but if you get worn out, it will be more difficult for you to keep up the good fight (see caregiver fatigue). I know you have probably already heard this, but it's true. Prayers for you both of you, for her continued healing, rest for you both, and peace for you both. God is doing a miraculous thing in how far she has come, and I pray for her recovery to continue, as a powerful testimony of God's Love.

It was no coincidence Shelley was getting better. The power of prayer was on full display. It was late by the time Keri and I got back to the hospital. Shelley was awake, she was excited because she knew we were coming, but couldn't remember why I had been gone most of the evening. Shelly was a real chatterbox, telling us how her friend Susan had come to visit for a while, and pastor Jason had come by and watched HGTV with her. She was upset the Texas Rangers had lost to Oakland, she felt like they had a pretty good team. What a premonition that was! Texas went on to win the World Series, and Shelley watched nearly every game through the entire season. She told me about how her Foley Catheter had come out, and her EVD had remained clamped all day, meaning her body was relearning how to regulate her ICP properly. Telling us all this wore her out though, and she was drifting off to sleep pretty quickly. Her daughter, Rachael, who had been staying with her while I was at my show, chastised me a little for not writing in the journal that was next to Shelley's bed that the family and guests had been writing in. I took a minute to jot a note.

Hey babe! Rachael has been teasing me that I have not written in the book. What she doesn't know is the ongoing conversation I have been having with you for seventeen days now. I have done my best to manage your care, the farm, our family, and somehow, we are keeping it all together. I don't understand in the slightest why this has happened to us, but we are in it together, no matter what. I begged God to bring you back, and He did, and He is providing us a path forward. I am ready for you to come home with me, because without you there, I have no desire to be home. We built our life together, and that's the only way I want to return to "life." I love you!

Saturday, April 22nd – Waves and Fog

Day 18 - I can't imagine how Shelley must feel. Every move she wants to make needs to be doctor approved and nurse assisted. She continues to make small steps forward clinically, but we struggle with sleeping at night and understanding the current limitations put on her by the doctors. We are hopeful that a couple more tubes come off today, including the EVD. That would improve things a lot.

I've been living here at the hospital with her for 18 days minus a few short trips to Walmart, the farm, and the shower. But I can't say that I can truly empathize with her position, because I can still get up and walk down the hall, eat some food, grab a Starbucks, or go sit outside for a minute. She can't do any of that, and I know it's tremendously discouraging.

I finally played a show last night, and had a great time, but walked away feeing guilty. She was supposed to be on that show with me. It's hard to find the heart to do it.

Sleep at night. Sleep at night. Pray it over and over. We need to get her body regulated so we can focus on improvements during the day.

Her sisters are back this weekend, let's hope that cheers her up a bit and gets us on the right path. Her Birthday is coming up on May 12th, and I think she definitely doesn't want to celebrate it here in the ICU.

UPDATE: CT scan showed too much swelling in the ventricles to remove the EVD. Will look again tomorrow.

．．．．

EIGHTEEN DAYS IN, AND a lot of people have said things like "I don't know how you are doing it." I know what they mean, and I usually reply, "Just taking it minute by minute." This is one hundred percent true. But there was another component, faith.

Faith is an interesting word and can mean a lot of things to a lot of people. It can be debated, discussed, argued, and thought of in a lot of different ways; but to me, it reminds me of a time when I was back in college.

My family and I spent most of our years boating on the Great Lakes around Michigan. Although he won't admit it, I was a much better pilot and navigator than my father, so when I was with my parents, I did most of the "driving." This particular instance, we were leaving Mackinac Island up in the Straits on our thirty-one-foot power boat. We motored on East and South to Cheboygan, where we stopped to take on fuel. The weather was near perfect, not a cloud in the sky, very little wind, and calm water. We left port and headed further down along the east coast of Michigan. As we left the protection the Straits provided, a strong North wind picked up, providing not only a substantial chop in the water, but some long rolling swells that were much bigger than they looked. I had to reduce speed, but we continued to plow our way through the rough water. We were really hoping to make it to Presque Isle, a beautiful little port tucked away in a small bay further down the coast. Out of nowhere, fog rolled in, so heavy that after a few minutes I could barely see the nose of the boat from the pilot's seat.

I throttled the boat back even further, we were barely moving at all, just creeping along at a couple miles an hour. The twin 460 big block V8 engines were loud in the cockpit, and there was no way we would be able to hear the bell or horn of other vessels, including the gigantic freighters that ran through these waters. After studying our charts, we decided to pull into the small state marina in Hammond Bay. It looked like we were fairly close, and it would get us out of danger. My dad went forward on the boat to listen for other vessels and see if he could pick out the buoy that marked the channel into the marina which was surrounded by shallow rocks. I put the coordinates into the Loran, and followed the directions precisely, keeping my heading and course as close as I could to its direction.

This was in the days long before GPS maps on our phones. A Loran provided you with your position, and by inputting the coordinates of your destination or target, a constantly updated heading you were supposed to take. My target was the buoy, for which we had the coordinates provided from our chart.

How does this relate to faith?

I needed to have faith that the chart was current and accurate, and that the buoy hadn't been moved or dragged into a new position. I had faith in the charts, they were a sailor's "bible." Much like the real Bible is our guide, we trust the words in it are true and accurate, the Word of God.

My dad, who was constantly questioning me from the front of the boat, needed to have faith that I was on the correct heading, updating my position, and adjusting my course accordingly. In this instance, metaphorically, I was the spiritual leader of our family. They had to trust I was interpreting the "word" correctly and guiding us appropriately.

After close to an hour of motoring slowly through rough water and the thickest fog I had ever seen, my dad started getting really nervous. Several times he asked me to turn back and head out into deeper water, afraid we had missed the buoy and would ground the boat, or worse, rip the bottom out on a jagged rock. I kept telling him to trust the chart and the electronics. It was the only way we would reach safety.

It materialized out of nowhere, a twelve-foot-tall shadow, rocking back and forth in the waves. I cranked the wheel to starboard and passed the buoy with just a few feet to spare. Later, my dad and I would talk about that experience and how we just needed to trust the charts and the "captain."

Faith.

I already knew my navigational chart was the Bible, but who was the captain? One might rush to assume that God is the captain, but in this case, that is not true. He created the chart, but is not the one guiding the ship. Maybe we could consider Jesus the captain? After all, He is our advocate for salvation, the One sent for us. But I think that still isn't quite right. In this example, Jesus is the electronics, the Loran that helps guide us based on the chart. Jesus is the way.

It wasn't the doctors or nurses; they were like the propulsion of the boat. It wasn't Shelley, she was a passenger on the boat. It was me. I needed to be the captain. I needed to interpret the charts, use my electronics to set the course, and guide my family to safety. In other words, I had to use the Word of God, my Bible. I had to have confidence in the doctors and nurses to propel us in the proper direction, a direction determined by prayer of where we were, and where we wanted to go. Then I had to have faith in that determination.

Faith.

It is easy to tell someone to have faith. But what we don't realize is that many people don't even know what faith really is. They are being told to believe in something they can't see, and therein lies the message God was wanting me to not only realize for myself, but to share with others.

Miracles still happen, but as a society we have diluted the importance of that word. If we still saw real miracles happening and gave glory to God for their occurrence, it would have a positive impact on our faith.

Miracles and faith.

It was all starting to make more sense to me. The past couple years, God had been giving us a platform, helping us build an audience. Now he was providing us with a miracle and wanted us to share it with the world. That vessel just needed a captain, and it looked like that was going to be me. Our first destination? Getting Shelley home.

Sunday, April 23rd – Overcomer

Day 19 - The EVD came out! This is a monumental step forward. It's also a little frightening, as we have had a way to drain excess fluid when her cranial pressure built up, but now it's up to her body to self-regulate that.

The doctors coming to see Shelley are all genuinely surprised at how well her progress is coming. Several times they have remarked on what a miracle in itself surviving this kind of hemorrhage is.

I saw my good friend and dueling piano partner, Tim Buie, praying for Shelley with the congregation at a church in the Bahamas. It is humbling to see how many people in so many places are thinking of her. I also was touched that my other dueling partner and mentor, Tom Basler, spent much of Friday evening making sure I was in a good place and praying with me before the show.

We still have a long road ahead of us, and there is still a danger of vasospasms, but there is light at the end of the tunnel and that's where we can focus our attention.

Finally, thank you Candida for the amazing artwork. Shelley had tears of joy when she saw it. We have some prints of it as well which we will be making available soon.

For the first time in almost three weeks, the ICU room is nearly silent. No chorus of beeps, chirping of alarms, and droning of pumps and fans. Maybe, Shelley can finally get a good night's sleep.

• • • •

I HAVE MENTIONED BEFORE that Shelley's daughter, Rachael, had been keeping a journal that people were asking to write in. There were a couple nice notes from the twenty-four-hour sitters that were on duty in her room.

Hey Shelley, this is Kimmie. I was a tech/sitter with you tonight. It was so nice to meet you and your kid sister and beautiful daughter. They were talking to me and telling me about your adventure, and I am absolutely amazed with your strength, willingness, and determination to overcome this. Then...they told me who you were! I was like OMG! No wonder she's kicking butt and taking names! You were an amazing woman and a force to be reckoned with during COVID and you are now! And to sit with you for twelve hours, I can tell you and God got this! I hope this note helps give you some gas on your tired days! Keep fighting sister! Love, PCT Kimmie

Overcome.

Shelley was on the road to overcoming this trial. Kimmie mentioned her strength, willingness, and determination. The willingness and determination were the tools she used to be obedient to God's direction. She had the faith to follow His guidance without question, and that was where she derived her strength from.

Miracles can and will happen. We must have faith and be obedient. Things were really starting to come into focus.

Isaiah 41:10 says, "So do not fear, for I am with you; do not be dismayed, for I am your God. I will strengthen you and help you; I will uphold you with my righteous right hand."

Fear.

That was the hardest thing for me to overcome. Fear of losing my wife. Fear of failing her family. Shelley had told me on several occasions she had no fear, even when in front of the judge that would imprison her, and in the face of the angry mob. She had no fear because she knew God would protect her. She had faith. She demonstrated for me exactly what things I needed to possess to overcome this with her.

One of the biggest challenges for Shelley at this point was to remain positive and upbeat, and not be stubborn with the doctors. She wanted to go home, but needed to get her EVD out, be cleared medically, and probably moved to some form of step-down unit for some physical therapy before they would even consider releasing her. This made her frustrated and angry at times, which would lead her to be stubborn with the doctors during neurological testing, who then were not confident she was ready to move on from the ICU.

I had a very serious discussion with her about this, and she promised me she would do her best when the doctors came in on this particular morning. When they entered to do testing during their morning rounds, Shelley was only mildly annoyed and was answering all their questions. One of the therapists was holding up different items around the room and asking Shelley to name them. Things like a cup, pencil, and blanket. She also pointed to several things around the room and asked Shelley to tell her what they were, things like the door, the television, and finally she pointed at the couch I was sitting on.

"What is your husband sitting on?"

Without missing a beat, Shelley answered with a grin and a touch of sarcasm in her voice.

"His ass."

The doctors and staff all chuckled, and it was decided Shelley was ready to have her EVD removed, and for her to really begin to do some physical therapy, including walking around the ICU floor.

"Look at what being a little pleasant gets you," I said after everyone left the room.

Shelley rolled her eyes and stifled a laugh.

"Babe, get my stuff. Let's get out of here."

Now it was my turn to roll my eyes. Soon, I thought to myself. We were getting really close.

Monday, April 24th – No Coincidences

Day 20 - It started a little scary today. There was some blood in the channel left behind by her EVD that they could see in the CT scan. That put a brief pause on everything while they decided what to do next. The consensus was to push on, and we were able to get the feeding tube out and Shelley ate her first meal. She started with the chocolate cake! Tomorrow we will begin the morning with another CT scan and check for blood.

We are getting very close to being able to move from the ICU to a PCU which is not as intensive care as the ICU, but still has a lot of medical supervision. It's another amazing step toward recovery.

My good friend Tim Buie called me today. We cried, we laughed, and we talked and he said something that I am not sure I've ever heard before. He said, "She walks in between the raindrops." I don't even know that I understand what he means by that, but metaphorically I love that picture, Shelley navigating her way through the storm without getting wet. I like to think she is that untouchable, she certainly displays that kind of resilience in the face of adversity, but this type of experience quickly reminded me that even the strongest can fall in battle.

A lot of the people who have reached out said "It's all in God's hands," or "Whatever happens is God's plan." But there have been a few that told me in one way or another their prayer wasn't "Thy will be done." Their prayer was more along the lines of "God, by the power of Your name she IS healed." That's something for me to ponder. Did all the prayer help to save and heal Shelley? Or was it God's plan for so many people to come together in prayer for something specific? Maybe it's both? I see the ripples spreading outward already from the affect this situation has had on people.

The weight of all this finally caught up with me today and I had a pretty solid cry. We have come so far, and we still have so far to go. Every day is another step. Today was the best day yet. I hope tomorrow is even better.

• • • •

BLOOD IN THE BRAIN. That was the big story of the day. It was showing up in all her scans. Her ventricles were not draining properly or there was a clot at the end of the channel left behind by the EVD spike in her head. The good news was that her cranial pressure was not exceeding the tolerable limits.

My friend, Tim Buie, called me today. He is a world class piano entertainer, one of the best I have ever seen. Arguably, he might be the best piano entertainer anyone has ever seen, and I have had the pleasure of doing dozens of dueling piano shows with him. It meant a lot to hear from him, and to know that the story of Shelley's incident and recovery was spreading all over the world. After hanging up, I was reminded of a moment Tim and I had shared while performing in Biloxi, Mississippi at the Beau Rivage.

To quickly put things into perspective, Tim and I were MGM Entertainment's featured act for the summer of 2018. They built an entire room for us at the Beau Rivage, and every night people waited for hours in line to come in and see us perform. On one particular night, it was extremely rowdy, even more than normal. A request crumpled up with a $100 dollar bill came flying across the piano to me from Tim, something he didn't want to do or didn't know. I opened it up and it was the Christian worship song "I Can Only Imagine" by Mercy Me.

Here was the conundrum. We ALWAYS play a $100 request, and unless there is a request with more money on it, that one is coming up next; however, we rarely play slow songs. The reason for this is slow songs can kill the buzz and excitement of the room. The last thing we want to do is drop the energy level in the room, so slow songs are very strategically placed if we feel the need to do them. Additionally, this was a worship song, in a room full of rowdy buzzed casino patrons. I clearly remember Tim was playing "Can't Take My Eyes Off You" by Frankie Valli and the crowd was on their feet singing the horn parts and chorus at the top of their lungs. We made eye contact, and Tim gave me a little affirmative head twitch that meant it was up to me.

I closed my eyes as Tim finished his song and started playing… "Don't Stop Believing." The crowd roared and the energy level rose even higher to an impossible level. They were singing every word.

I had chickened out. As I wrapped up my song, Tim launched into "Great Balls of Fire." This was a signature song for us that had us switching pianos, alternating solos, and really tearing the place up. Back in the days before safety became an issue, we may or may not have lit the pianos on fire with some flammable liquid. My point is the place was a madhouse. As we finished the song, Tim was looking across the piano, but not at me, he was looking at the $100 bill with his eyebrows raised, as if to say, you better do it.

It was against every instinct that I had as a performer. I closed my eyes again, and this time launched into the unmistakable introduction that has been played in every contemporary church in the United States. The room hushed instantly.

I kept my eyes closed and played and sang. I was no stranger to the song; I had led it numerous times in worship, and I gave it my all. I could hear people singing along with it, but not at the level they had the previous couple songs. As I finished, I opened my eyes. The entire room was on their feet, many with hands in the air and eyes closed, and the applause and cheering as the last notes died away were every bit as loud as they had been for "Great Balls of Fire."

At the end of the night, a middle-aged couple walked up to us at the pianos and thanked us for playing the worship song. There were tears in their eyes.

"We lost our daughter one year ago today, and that was the song we had them play at her funeral. Thank you so much for playing that tonight."

I had a hard time going to sleep that night, wondering why I had tried to skip the song, and was amazed at the reception it got when I decided to play it. I should have had the courage to do it in the first place.

Back in the present, as I walked back to the hospital room, I wondered why God had urged Tim Buie to call me, and why that moment with him had been replayed so vividly in my mind. One thing I knew for certain, there are no coincidences, and God had previously taught me a lesson that had an application now or in the near future.

That night I had a hard time getting to sleep on the couch. I was bothered by the meaning of the song and why it was so heavy in my mind. For the song writer, Bart Millard, it was a song inspired by the pain, redemption, and healing brought about by the transformation God made in the life of his once abusive father. For many others, like that couple in Biloxi, it was a song of mourning the loss of a loved one. Even more troubling to me, was that Shelley had often asked me to lead that song when we were leading worship together. There was something God was wanting me to unpack here, but I just was not getting it.

If only God would fill out request slips.

Tuesday, April 25th – Building Blocks

Day 21 - Three weeks…it's a long time to be in the ICU, and Shelley is determined to be done with it as soon as possible. The parade of doctors and nurses stopping by to see how well she is doing makes me feel like we are animals in a zoo a little bit. But I have to admit, she is breaking every record, spoiling every prediction, and making it known she wants to go home.

Pray for wisdom, patience, discernment, and a steady pace.

. . . .

EVERY DOCTOR THAT COMES into the room looks surprised. Shelley has managed to improve and heal up to a point where most of her wires, tubes, and other accessories are removed. She walks around the ICU floor, gets up to use the bathroom on her own, and loves bossing everyone around.

She is also a terrible patient.

I say that in the most loving way, of course. She is hyper-focused on getting out of the hospital, and every doctor and therapist is trying to explain to her why that is a bad idea right now. This makes her extremely agitated, she gets frustrated with the doctors, and finally shuts herself down in a world of self-pity and anger. What we will not discover until months later is she had no idea what was going on and has no recollection of her hospital stay at all. We all assumed since her eyes were open and she was talking, Shelley was back.

Not quite.

"God, give Shelley the patience she needs for her body to prepare itself to go home."

Shelley also is not eating like the doctors expected or wanted her to. Her sense of taste is all messed up and nothing tastes good to her. It is not for a lack of trying though, she is ordering everything on the menu, hoping something will work for her taste buds. The doctors and therapist told her she needed to eat several complete meals before they would feel comfortable releasing her.

"God, provide a steady pace of recovery for my wife."

There is a picture our friend Rebecca posted of Shelley taking a walk around the ICU floor, tethered to a nurse with a caption that reads: Be the kind of woman that when your feet hit the floor each morning the devil says, "Oh crap, she's up!" It had 1400 likes, 260 comments, 140 shares, and 18,989 views.

"God, give me the wisdom to reach these people with the words You want them to hear."

The hate was starting to build on social media. Her recovery was triggering some that had hoped for a different outcome. I am choosing not to breathe more life into their words by rewriting them in this book, but it was sad to see and read the hate some people had for a woman who had nearly died and was appearing to recover.

"God, give me the power of discernment, so that I can keep my wife safe from those wishing her harm."

Keri had written a much better social media update than me the day before and I saw it reposted in the prayer chain group.

Shelley is the strongest person I know. A lot of people say that, but she is proving that every minute of the day. Let's start with more prayers answered!!

She passed her swallow test and ate half a grilled cheese sandwich!!! Thank you, Jesus!!

She stood and walked around!! Thank you, Jesus!

She passed her cognitive test and is speaking like a champ! She has a little trouble with some word recall, but refuses to let us help her and she will try and try and try until the word comes to her!! Thank you, Jesus!

I gave her a pen and she signed her name as beautifully as she normally does! Thank you, Jesus!!

She brushed her teeth by herself for the 1st time! Thank you, Jesus!!

Both her left and right arms and legs seem to be equal in strength!!!! Thank you, Jesus!!

Now for the prayer requests...

This morning, we got a bit of discouraging news that when they removed the brain drain (there is an actual name, but I prefer the visual description) a small trail of blood showed on the CT scan. I PRAY her body is able to absorb this and it doesn't get out of control again and her CT scan shows improvement tomorrow.

I pray her headaches stay to a minimum as her brain heals, and then they stop completely.

I pray her vocabulary continues to get strong and she continues to work hard.

I pray the 3am ICU deliriums stop. She wants to leave the hospital at this time every day and gets really frustrated. I pray she can sleep through the night.

I hope Shelley's story has reminded many of how hope and the power of prayer to God and positivity can heal all things.

There is no other way to explain life support with a bleeding aneurysm to talking, laughing and walking eight days later.

She is a miracle, and all praise goes to Our Heavenly Father who is letting us know Shelley was not done yet. Her message is strong, and she hasn't even begun to speak on it yet.

Thank you all for your continued prayers. I pray her message has spread hope country wide and that with God, ANYTHING is possible.

Keep believing!

Hope.

That is an interesting word. Its definition is a feeling of expectation and desire for a certain thing to happen. Another version of the definition is desire accompanied by expectation of or belief in fulfillment. A deeper dive into the word hope biblically reveals we need to have faith to have hope. Hebrews 10:22-23 says ...let us draw near to God with a sincere heart and with the full assurance that faith brings, having our hearts sprinkled to cleanse us from a guilty conscience and having our bodies washed with pure water. Let us hold unswervingly to the hope we profess, for he who promised is faithful.

Earlier in this book, I discussed my metaphor for faith by describing piloting my dad's boat into the harbor blindly during bad weather. We were all hoping we were going to make it; however, we had to have more than hope. The faith provided by the tools we had at our disposal were ultimately what gave us hope.

The hope we had for Shelley's survival was built on the faith we had in prayer. Thinking back to pastor Jason's message, "Guarding the Garden," I was not just protecting her physically, I was protecting her spiritually. If my message had been one of defeat, if I had asked for prayers for Shelley's comfort when the doctor told me she wouldn't make it, would the outcome have been different?

If prayer really matters, I would think so. The pieces were starting to come together and make more sense to me. The building blocks of the miracle that was happening in front of my eyes were becoming clearer. We were going through a time of trial and refinement, but why and for what reason I still did not know.

Wednesday April 26th - Hero

Day 22 - Three years ago, today, I watched something pretty amazing take place. When Shelley stepped up onto this podium she started off by telling everyone she was nobody special. From the back of the crowd somebody yelled, "We needed a hero!" And from that day forward our lives were changed - dramatically.

A friend of ours sent this to me yesterday and I wanted to share it:

"There are many people that look at Shelley as a larger-than-life hero that stood up when no one else would. That is undoubtably true and an awesome testament to her strength and courage. I place Shelley on my own short list of three Texas women that really made a difference for freedom in Texas in the last few decades!

But the regular person side of Shelley is awesome too! Over the last few weeks, one thing that keeps coming to my mind is my 50th "surprise" birthday party. When we were watching the video clips compiled of friends hacking on me and sometimes saying too nice of things, Shelley explicitly turned around many times during the clips to see how I was reacting. I think she wanted to see how this low-key introvert might react to the words of lifelong friends and new "foxhole" friends coming together to celebrate. I know she wanted to see my emotions bubble over a little and maybe she did. She was fully engaged in the human element of it and that has stuck with me since then. I realize this is a minor example, but I think it's pretty sound in showing how important person-to-person connections are to her and that her often overlooked softer side is also inspiring.

Anyway, I just wanted to share that with you because I think sometimes the hero Shelley is so "bigger-than-life" that the regular person Shelley doesn't get the recognition that is deserved. I do

know that this human-engaged side is broadly apparent to those that are fortunate enough to consider her a friend."

We have been so blessed by so many people as we walk this path in our lives right now, and I like to think it's because of the way she has given of herself to everyone like our friend wrote about above. Undoubtedly Shelley is a hero to many people, but many more call her friend, and I can't personally thank any of you enough for all the prayers and support you are giving.

Tonight let's pray for two things. No more headaches and a clear CT scan. If we can get past those two things, we are going to witness another miracle.

· · · ·

BEING SECULAR MUSICIANS together was easy. People either liked what we did, or they didn't. They packed the dance floor and filled all the seats in the house, or they moved on to some other form of entertainment. We had a formula we used to select the songs, we had personalities we wore on stage, and for most people, it worked. If they didn't like us or our music, it was no big deal!

Being thrust into the public eye changed all that. Half the world loved her stand for freedom, half the world literally wanted to kill her for it. Nobody wants to be a hero in those circumstances. In fact, people seeking to become heroes rarely, if ever, achieve that status. Heroes are created by people's reaction to an individual's actions, particularly in the face of adversity. Shelley never wanted to be a hero, but things happened and there we were, with a spotlight shining on us. For several years we thought that was supposed to be the big moment in our lives. Now I was not so sure. I was beginning to suspect that moment was more of a preparatory stage. God had been building a platform for us, and we needed to figure out what to do with it. Experiencing a miracle with so many people praying and watching was great, but I knew that was not the mission laid out for us.

Shelley's recovery was steady but painful. She was still hallucinating a lot, and she was experiencing some serious pain in her head from a hardened blood clot left behind from the EVD. She was also miserable in the ICU, and wanted nothing more than to leave. The doctors had told me the plan was to step her down to a regular hospital floor as soon as they felt she was ready so she could get better access to therapy and continue on the path of leaving the hospital. I was not sure she was going to go for that. In her mind, once they let her leave the ICU, she was going home.

I sent the following text in our family group chat.

She did so well with PT yesterday they are considering outpatient therapy and sending her home if she has twenty-four-hour supervision by a family member, and commits to three days of outpatient therapy a week. I think we are getting close here. Several teams have signed off on her. Waiting for Neuro or stroke team to feel one hundred percent about her brain drain channel healing up and no increase in swelling. She has a dull headache this morning, but they gave her some meds for it.

"Nurse Keri" had been hard at work getting her sister to walk, eat, and complete her therapy regimen. I have said it before, but I honestly don't know if I would have made it without her. Her social media post really touched me emotionally that night.

Shelley's sister said it best tonight.

Thank you all for the continued prayers!!!

20 days ago my life changed forever. I have felt emotions that I did not know existed throughout my whole body. Down, down, down, up, down, up, down, up, up UP!

I'm telling yall now...please call your family and friends and share how much they mean to you. I had to tell my sister while she was on life support and it hit me, why didn't I tell her more?? My sister was invincible to me. NEVER did I think I would lose her. Not til we were at least 90! She's a powerhouse, my lighthouse, my

rock and literally half my heart. God gave me a big dose of humility and remembering to trust in Him.

To see her shake, struggle and deteriorate right before my eyes and I could do nothing is something I never want ANY OF YOU to ever feel. So, for Shelley's sake...call your mom and dad, your siblings or that long lost friend and let them know just how important they are to you.

Shelley is killing the game!! So much, that she may be discharged from NICU in a few days!!!! What!?!??! Seriously!! Thank you Jesus!!

What I pray for today is that she has patience and slows her roll a little. She is such a fighter that she wants to be 100% now! Admirable yes, yet not having food and literally being on life support 10 days ago, Patience.... we need the calming voice of Jesus to help her to rest and recovery.

Her brain bleed is still slightly there, so we pray that goes away!!

I pray for her speech to continue to improve and for her word find to become easier and less frustrating.

I pray she can feel all the love and support from across the nation.

I pray for a financial miracle to help with the overwhelming medical bills that have begun to pile up, as well as what's to lie ahead.

I pray the stent and flow valve in her brain continue to supply blood and oxygen to their appropriate locations.

I pray that her story has touched someone that may have been wavering on questioning Gods grace and his ability to heal even the sickest person. HE CAN AND HE WILL!!

YOU MUST BELIEVE with EVERY CELL in your body. I know I do, and I will spend my days sharing this story to help those that don't. Her testimony will be heard and that is all God asks in return. Simple and done!

Thank you thank you thank you!!!

Yall have helped me through the toughest days of my life to date with your prayers and beautiful messages of hope and love.

My children thank you for helping to bring their aunt back. Moving to chapter two of a beautiful testimony to God and all his believers!!

Keep BELIEVING!!

The paragraph about telling your family and friends what they mean to you now was especially heavy. God was really highlighting that for me, but not because I didn't do it. Losing my mom had reinforced that for me a long time ago. Instead, it was like He was highlighting that as part of the message that needed to get out.

While I was sitting in the dark contemplating all this late that night, I heard Shelley's raspy voice call out from her bed.

"Hey babe, get my stuff and let's get out of here."

I could not agree more.

Thursday, April 27th – Going Home

Day 23 - We had one of our toughest nights yet. Headaches, nausea, whole body pain, lack of appetite. She was miserable. But two different CT scans came back all clear, and after conferring with her team, the doctors decided the best move to help jumpstart her body was to send her home. So, we came home. Praise the Lord!

So what's next? We need to find an appetite. Conquer the anxiety and fear of being free of the doctors and nurses. Sounds crazy, but when something wasn't feeling right, someone was always right there. Now it's all on our own shoulders. Physical therapy, occupational therapy, and speech therapy. Doctor's appointments, follow up appointments, more scans and tests. Our job for a while is going to be survival and recovery.

I'm very happy to finally have my wife home. For everyone who prayed for us, thank you. The survival rate of the hemorrhage she suffered is not very good, and we beat those odds. But we still have a long way to go, and tonight I'm praying for a relaxed night of sleep in the bed that's been empty for the last three weeks.

· · · ·

THE UPDATE LEFT OUT a lot of critical details. The night had been horrific. Hallucinations, nausea, and severe body pain were making Shelley miserable. They took her for CT scans two different times, and the doctor told me that he believed the blood clot was causing issues in the ventricle, and that blood in her spinal fluid was also causing a lot of discomfort. The scans came back, and amazingly the blood clot was gone. Completely.

Every doctor, nurse, and therapist on her team came in to see her that morning, and Shelley was a mess. She was in tears begging to be go. She wanted nothing more than to go home, and at one point she kicked everyone out of the room except me and begged me to take her home. She did not want to die in the ICU, and if she stayed there any longer, that was what was going to happen.

I met with her entire team out in the hallway. The discussion lasted close to thirty minutes while everybody signed off on her release. It came down to one thing. She needed to eat lunch. If she could do that, she could go. She was dangerously thin and suffering from malnutrition, and would not have the luxury of a feeding tube at home.

I went back into the room and relayed the news to her. I thought she would be happy. Instead, she started to panic, and so did I. We had become dependent on the nurses, the medication, the care, the doctors – all of it. If something didn't feel right, we always had a nurse there to check vitals, order medication, or call for a scan or doctor. Suddenly, we were going to be on our own.

It was just the two of us in the room. I got down on my knees next to the bed, held her hand, and started praying. "God, you would not have brought us this far just to fail. It is time for us to go home. Give Shelley the strength to get out of this bed. Give me the wisdom to care of her when we get home. Protect us like you always have, Father. We trust You, we have faith in where You are leading us, and we will be obedient to Your call. And God, please give Shelley an appetite so these doctors will let us leave."

I thought I was pretty clever for trying to inject a little humor into the end of the prayer, and I looked up at my wife. She already had the room service menu open and was reaching for the phone to call.

Every nurse and every doctor came to see Shelley that day. It took me a long time to pack up all the cards, crosses, stuffed animals, and other gifts people had brought that were spread out throughout the room. Even though I triple checked everything, I ended up leaving behind the black sweatpants and pink sweatshirt that she had worn to the hospital on April 4th. It took nearly all day to check out of the hospital which was frustrating Shelley immensely. But by about 4:00

PM, we were loading up into my truck and starting our journey home. Shelley took out her phone and sent a text message on the family group chat.

I'm long way fast going long.

Just to help everyone understand I translated the text.

That's code for she's going home.

After sending that text, Shelley put her phone down, curled into a ball in the passenger seat and began to sob. There was nothing I could do to console her or make her feel better. For the first time since this journey began, I watched my wife really cry. It was the one of the most heart-breaking things I had seen in the past month. I could not even begin to imagine what she was feeling or thinking. I just put my hand on her side and did my best to get her home as quickly as possible.

Several times she asked me if I was taking her home. Every time I told her yes, her crying would intensify. I think the seriousness of the situation and the trauma she had been through finally had caught up with her. Everyone was waiting for us at the house when we arrived. She hugged everyone, smiling through her tears, then asked me to come in the bedroom with her. She curled up in my arms and almost immediately fell asleep, the first time in twenty-three days we were able to cuddle up on a bed together.

Thank you, God, for giving me my wife back.

Friday, April 28th – There's No Place Like Home

Day 24 - The past 24 hours have been the most restful Shelley has had. Being in familiar surroundings and the comfort of home has really helped her anxiety and almost totally eliminated the delirium she was experiencing in the ICU. We were able to eat three small meals and take a shower which was a huge relief after over three weeks without one. Just that little amount of activity was also exhausting and really showed us how much work there is to do.

We are shifting into a new phase of this journey. Instead of a survival or rescue situation, we are now in a recovery and rehabilitation stage. For now that means 24 hour supervision, taking all the right medication at the right time, and working on finding the energy to eat and move around a little bit. It's a full day all in itself.

A little progress every day. That's what I'm praying for. Hopefully each day will be a little better than the last, and even when we slip backwards a little bit, there will still be positives to hold on to.

I got a good glimpse of our little Joey today while feeding the Roos. Shelley has not had the energy yet to see most of the animals. The dogs have all given her a lot of kisses, and we showed her a couple of the baby chicks. She can see the horses out the back windows, and I can't wait for her to be able to get back out and see the rest of her animal family.

. . . .

BEING HOME FELT AMAZING. We still had a long way to go. I realized Shelley was not as strong as she had looked in the hospital, and the amount of medication she needed to take was overwhelming. She was able to take a shower with a lot of assistance, and most of her first night and the next day were spent in bed. I was able to catch up with all the animals on the farm, and even mow the grass which had not been touched since I had given it a first cutting at the beginning of April.

I knew things were not going to be easy, but I was not prepared for the level of care Shelley was going to require. She had also fooled us with her appetite at the hospital. Nothing tasted good to her, and she did not want to eat. I figured I would give her a day or two to sort it out in her own head before panicking too much.

For me, it was the first time I could really sleep comfortably. I had been trying to sleep mostly on an uncomfortable ICU couch or in a chair for the past twenty-three nights. Even with alarms set throughout the night to check vitals and give Shelley medication, I felt more rested and comfortable than I had in a long time.

Plenty of family was still around, and we were home where we belonged. Dare I say, end of story?

Saturday, April 29th – Not End of Story

Day 25 - Shelley decided she wanted to watch the Rangers/Yankees game tonight on TV. When I asked if she wanted some "baseball food" for the game, she thought about it for a while and then sent me to Sonic. One corn dog, large onion rings, large tots; all extra crispy, and a Butterfinger Blast with some extra caramel.

What?

She hadn't had more than a nibble in days. This is a big step! Pain management has been pretty successful so far. I think I have mastered the medication schedule. It was another day of mostly sleep and rest, some time with family this afternoon, and then watching the baseball game on TV tonight.

I think the decision to come home is paying off. General wellness seems much better. Next week, we will start working on all the rehab and therapy. We still need to go get some staples removed from her head, and follow up with the surgeon to check on the flow diverter that was inserted into her carotid artery.

Other than a few select shows, I'm taking the month of May off. The Piano Man Experience will be at The Frisco StrEATs festival and Potosi Live, and I've got several engagements with Windbreakers, Killer Dueling Piano's, and solo. Most of my time will be taking care of business at home. We have a lot of animals that need care, a baby Roo that's ready to come out of the pouch, and trying to find some rhythm and balance as we progress with recovery.

. . . .

THERE WAS AN ADDITIONAL post I made that day, and I initially wasn't going to include it, but God told me to address it. It had to do with several comments and conversations people made on social media about Shelley.

Did she make it?

I hope she gets to meet her lord and savior.

Shelley Luther, owner of the plague rat salon in Dallas, suffered a brain aneurysm. First Trump was indicted on 34 felony counts and now this. I might just start believing in god again. #holyweek2023 #ibelieveinmiracles #godsplan #godsplanisperfect

Let's all be grateful Shelley is resting. May she soon rest in peace.

There were more posts, all similar in nature, but those should give you an idea of what was being said. My extra post was as follows:

I think it's people like this that are slowly destroying humanity. When it becomes socially acceptable to wish death on someone and ridicule their struggle to recover, we've lost our way as a species. It's morally reprehensible, not only for the person posting, but for those that want to promote this person's post with comments and support. Now I know a lot of you will say ignore, block, delete - but let me ask you, if someone was saying these things about a family member of yours, is it really that easy to scroll on by and ignore? Let's go one step further, when Shelley is able to pick up a phone or tablet and look through social media, what effect is seeing something like that going to have on her? The last three years have made us pretty disciplined and thick skinned, but I don't know that anyone who's gone through what she has wants to subjected to that. Social media has given a lot of people a false sense of bravado, I'm guessing most of them would crumble under the pressure of an actual crisis. That's what made Shelley different, like her or not, agree with her or not, you have to admit she stood her ground in the toughest of times. If she ever sees this, she will probably ask me why I even wasted my time. My answer is because sometimes I just

can't let something roll off my back, not when they are attacking you when you are defenseless.

Guarding my Garden again, I suppose. Seriously though, what in the world is wrong with people? I feel like I could write up a really long rant about how social media has made people's tongues pure evil and filth; but that is not the point of this book. I do, however, feel compelled to share the hatred some people had for what we were going through and call it out for what it is. Spiritual warfare.

Seeing responses like this only hardened my resolve to figure out why we were placed into this position. God's plan was big enough to stir opposing forces up against us.

Sunday, April 30th – Slow and Steady

Day 26 - Another day of small but steady progress. A little less time sleeping, a little more time eating, watched the Rangers game on TV. We even took a short walk around the front yard in the sun today.

Still working on finding an appetite. Her sense of smell is off a bit, and that seems to be troublesome, and her sense of taste is really off. But she is trying hard to try and get some food down.

Rhythm and routine are important right now. Trying to sleep through the night, making sure we have some sort of activity, even if it's brief, during the day. Eating regular meals, getting medication on time, getting enough liquid. Trying to make a phone call or two, sending a text or two - these seemingly simple tasks require a lot of focus and energy. But we are attempting to do that, and it's always nice to hear the surprise in someone's voice or get a happy text back.

Finally feel like the house is getting back to normal. After being gone for over three weeks it felt strange at first. We are so thankful for all the family and close friends that have helped us out. Praying for another small step forward tomorrow!

 • • • •

BEING HOME FROM THE hospital, while a relief, was tough. Shelley required a lot of care and observation. We were blessed to have a lot of family still taking turns visiting and helping. Shelley was not ready to go to church yet, being in public was frightening to her, but we were getting spiritually fed by our pastor Jason and his wife, Molly.

You have heard me mention our friend, Rebecca Sprouse, who brought Shelley the prayer shawl. I can't tell you how many times she came to the hospital, even knowing there would be times she would not be able to go into the ICU room. She organized prayer vigils, and even started a Facebook group called Prayer Chain for Shelley Luther. To this day she still posts prayers in it almost daily, and there are over five-hundred members that share testimony, prayer, and God's word. I encourage you to find it and join, you will be immeasurably blessed. Becca was constantly checking in through text, stopping by with little things we needed, and helping in ways I didn't even know we needed. Without Becca, I don't know that Shelley would have made it. She was one of the catalysts that sparked the huge outpouring of positive thoughts and prayer.

Day 27 - Today Shelley asked me if she had two separate aneurysms. When I asked what she meant, she told me she remembers having the first one, going to the hospital, then coming home for a while, then having another one and going back into the hospital again. After discussing this for a while, we settled on the idea that while in a coma, she was dreaming that she was home. Waking up in a different hospital than the one we started in fit in with her dream, making her feel like she had gotten sick twice. At first this seemed ok, and I told her that it was much better for her to have had pleasant dreams of being at home than it was to have memories of being in the hospital like that. However, as her mind absorbed this, she became anxious that maybe she was still in a dream now, and that perhaps she was still in a coma in the hospital. It reminded me of the movie, Inception, where the characters needed a little marker or mind trick that they would use to determine if they were in a dream or not. Shelley woke me up several times throughout the night to check if she was dreaming or if this was real. This is definitely a wrinkle I wasn't expecting. The way she described the dream seems that it was vivid and real enough to assume it was real. When I dream, I almost always know that it's a dream and can work myself out of it. I'm guessing when one is in a coma, if they are dreaming, they can't wake up from it, and to their brain the memory of it seems that much more tangible.

We are celebrating Logann's birthday tonight, and Shelley says she is craving one of the steaks on the grill. I am hopeful we are turning the corner on the loss of appetite.

We made a few more phone calls and texts today. That brings her joy, although finding the right words is sometimes a little frustrating.

All in all another day of little improvements. I'll take it!

. . . .

DAY 28 - WE HAD A TOUGH night last night. I think the dosage of her meds are off just a little bit. The daytime nerve blockers wear off a little early, forcing us to take the nighttime block a little early, and we just can't get in the comfort zone. After talking to the doctor, we are trying a little change to see if we can get better coverage throughout the day so we can take the nighttime meds at a later hour.

We are watching the Rangers while eating a little Cowboy Chicken tonight with family. We might switch over to the Stars game if Shelley stays awake long enough. Little moments feel almost normal at times. I am so thankful for that. I'm hoping we get to take in a Rangers game in person this year.

We had over sixty baby chicks born while Shelley was in the hospital, and all of them have made it. So the next couple days will be spent expanding our chicken runs and getting ready for them to move outside. Our baby roo is ready to be pulled from her mom's pouch as well. Lots of fun on the farm! Finally feel like I'm getting control of the yard and the animals again.

Thanks again to everyone for all the prayers, love, and support.

. . . .

DAY 29 - SHELLEY SPENT a while this afternoon making a Facebook post. She will be the first to tell you that typing and figuring out words is hard for her right now. But after a while she hashed out what she wanted to say and posted it. A few minutes later she was crying.

Now I was prepared for this, and I was figuring we were about to have the "Why did this happen to me?" conversation. We have not had this conversation, but I assumed she was upset with having to struggle with simply posting on social media.

I was wrong.

She told me she felt unworthy of all the prayers and support people were sending. She just wanted to post something because she felt bad and thought everyone would be upset that she was ignoring them. She said she didn't deserve all the positive thoughts people were sending her way.

We talked about it for a long time, and I'm not sure I helped her one bit. But this is what I know and told her.

God often chooses people who think they are the most unworthy, not because they are truly unworthy, but because the humbleness and trueness of their heart makes them feel that way. She has blessed so many people in her life, she deserves every blessing she is getting back right now.

We had a good day today, but we are still struggling to figure everything out. As the seriousness of this experience settles in, it stirs up fear and anxiety. Praying for peace and comfort in those times.

. . . .

DAY 30 - WE MADE A nice step forward today. She had a good appetite, took a little walk around the farm, had a nice visit with family and friends, and stayed relatively pain free all day. Thank you, Jesus!

We spent a long time today talking with our friend Judy about miracles. Using the word miracle really comes with a lot of responsibility. As we reminisced about what happened, what the doctors said, and where we came from, I have no doubt a miracle has and is still taking place.

I think that's where I'm leaving it tonight. Miracle is a really big word, and it gives me a lot to think about.

. . . .

DAY 31 - I SPENT MOST of the day working out on the farm. We are lucky to have Shelley's mom and daughter here right now to help so I can try and get caught up on the animals.

Her appetite continues to improve, and I think Shelley is going to be ready physically to begin PT and attend doctor appointments.

Keeping it simple tonight - watching the Rangers game.

• • • •

DAY 32 - UPDATE COMES a little early today. I'm playing a show at the Frisco Rail Merchants StrEATs Festival. Normally, Shelley is on these shows with me. We are better on stage together, and it's tough not having my partner with me. It's also stressful, even though there is family with her at the house, it's the first time I am going to be away for more than a short while since she has been home from the hospital. This is part of the learning process for me as I am going to have to find a way to support our family for a while on my own until she heals, and we are able to assess what our next life steps will be together. I can tell she is feeling disappointed, or that she has let me down today, and it doesn't matter how much I try to convince her that's not true, she will feel that way because that's the way her heart has been for me since day one. If you read this update today, Shelley, I am only here and able to do this because of the support and confidence you have had in me. You've fought for me since you've known me, now let me fight for you!

Three years ago today also marks the first full day Shelley spent in jail for keeping the salon open. It's also the only day she has ever truly been mad at me. Hannity wanted her on TV, but since she couldn't be there, I was the next best thing. She told me if it had been Tucker I might have become a casualty of that whole mess. The truth is, those couple of years made us closer to one another than I could have ever imagined.

Next week is a big week for us. Three doctors' appointments, the beginning of true PT, OT, and ST, staples coming out of her head, and finally not only is it Mother's Day, it's also her birthday! It will definitely be a test of her energy and stamina.

Thank you all for your prayers. If you are around Frisco today, stop by and see me between 5:30 and 7:00pm on the main stage!

. . . .

DAY 33 - THANK YOU to everyone who went to the POB event today. Even though I could only stop by for a few minutes it was very special to see all of you.

For the rest of you, I'll reiterate what I told the attendees at today's event - Don't waste one day. Wake up every morning ready to take on whatever challenge lies ahead. Because one day, you might not wake up. Or you might wake up with new unpredicted challenges. Don't wait for the day after tomorrow. That could be a day too late.

As Shelley continues to improve, she continues to reveal more of what she remembers and experienced, and I can't wait for her to start sharing that with you. It's her story to tell, I'm simply a witness to a miracle that I'll forever be thankful for.

. . . .

DAY 34 - TODAY WE TOOK a little test drive in the car to see if we can handle the drive to the doctor appointments tomorrow. All went pretty well. Tomorrow will be our busiest day since coming home from the hospital. Two doctor visits and the staples come out of her head.

Papa Byrd is coming back to town tomorrow. Cherry pie anyone? If you know, you know.

Watching the Rangers game again tonight. That's become our thing. We both love baseball, and it appears the Rangers are going to give us something to cheer for this year. Another miracle!

The next few days are going to tell us a lot. Hope we are ready for it!

• • • •

DAY 35 - "I DON'T KNOW how people can live without faith." That's what the PA said at one of the doctor's offices today. After the experiences this past month, I not only agree, but must ask, what else is there?

Both appointments went well, and the staples and stitches are out of her head. Every visit with a health professional only reinforces the fact that we are extremely lucky.

Every day I wonder if this will be my last update, and then I get another message from a friend of a friend of a friend who heard our story and now is having conversations with their child, parent, or friend about their faith.

I think I'll keep posting for a while. What started as a simple way to update people and allow me some emotional venting has evolved into something more. I have faith it's doing good.

• • • •

DAY 36 - TODAY WAS a day of rest and recovery after two doctor's appointments yesterday. Her appetite continues to improve, and we seem to have pain management under control for the most part. So now it's working on regaining strength and language skills.

I'm developing a routine with the animals, but I'm way behind in the yard, garden, and pastures. The first batch of chickens that hatched the night we went to the hospital are now out in their coop. All of them made it. That's a miracle all its own!

We have been spending a lot of time talking about the time in the hospital, and what happened while we were there. It's difficult at times trying to explain everything that was happening without worrying about it being too much. It's also hard to believe this all started just over five weeks ago.

. . . .

DAY 37 - WE HAD OUR best night of sleep since leaving the hospital. That's positive. We struggled with some head and neck pain this afternoon, but were able to get it under control with medication.

The really BIG news was our female roo, Willow, gave us a beautiful little female joey. I'm hoping she will be a therapeutic addition to Shelley's routine. Most of the joey's day for the next few weeks is being held and bottle fed as we try to socialize her with humans.

We have been getting a lot of people asking when Shelley will be singing again. I pray it's soon! However, we have a really long road ahead of us, and it's probably going to be quite a while before we are at that point.

Trying to stay awake long enough to watch the Rangers and then catch the tail end of the Stars game. Any suggestions for names for our new roo?

. . . .

DAYS 38 THROUGH 40 - It's been a busy weekend. Shelley's sisters came to town for her birthday on Friday. We had a lot to celebrate, but it was also a little bittersweet for Shelley. One doesn't expect to be celebrating recovering from an aneurysm, hemorrhage, and stroke for your 50th birthday. Every day is a little better, a little improvement, and another step ahead.

Thinking back three years ago, Shelley was still pretty fresh out of jail, and I remember Sarah Palin calling to wish her a happy Mother's Day. We have had quite a journey since then, and I was certainly not ready for it to be over. As every day goes by, we get a little more comfortable talking about the days in the hospital while she was in a coma, and the emotions surrounding those days when the future was so uncertain.

This next week we will start some therapy and continue to strive for improvements in pain management, strength and stamina, and speech. Caregiving is a full-time commitment, and people's generosity has been a huge help and blessing to allow me the privilege of being able to care for my wife. I am slowly adding (keeping) a few shows back to the schedule as long as we have some family in town to help.

We hope everyone had a blessed Mother's Day!

· · · ·

DAYS 40-45 I HAVEN'T written much lately because every day is pretty much the same. Wake up, take medication, follow up on a doctor's appointment, watch the ballgame, short visit with family or close friend, take medication, and go to bed. We see little signs of improvement every day that keeps us feeling positive.

There is definitely a lot of apprehension about what the future is going to be like. We don't know where Shelley's recovery is going to land, and how long it will take. I don't think anyone is ready to make major unplanned life changes at age 50. There seems to be less anxiety every day, but imagine wondering if every little twinge of a headache is going to send you back to the ICU in an ambulance.

Learning how to deal with the unknown and with this fear is our biggest challenge right now. It's definitely an exercise or test of faith. I thought the hard test was the first few days in the hospital, but maybe the recovery period is the real trial. One thing I'm sure of, even after the past six weeks, God is still teaching me lessons.

Anyone who knows our horses understand they are all rescues. This means they went to auction and didn't sell because there was something wrong with them. They have a sickness, an injury, a bad temperament, there is no telling what you are getting from the kill pen.

There is a lease pasture behind our acreage that houses several horses that are the opposite of ours. They look like they are straight off the set of a Wyatt Earp movie with strong bloodlines and no afflictions or ailments to speak of. The recent storms broke one of the fences on the lease pasture and those horses were grazing in our neighbor's yard. They checked with us to see if any of them were ours and while I wished they were I said no, and they eventually got in touch with the owner. The next day, as I was feeding our horses, I noticed one of the neighbor's horses was up grazing with ours, and I grabbed a lead rope, played cowboy for a moment to round him up, then took him for a walk to take him back to his lease. He was a beautiful buckskin, fat in all the right spots, muscles rippling in his shoulders and flanks, and a perfect coat. It made me a little sad because it was exactly the horse Shelley had always wanted. In fact, we had recently rescued a buckskin that had an incredibly hard winter. He wouldn't eat hay, had some sort of stomach ulcers that irritated him so bad he could only eat green grass, specialized food, and take medication that was $600 every thirty days. I had nursed him through the winter, but he had remained looking like a skeleton, all his ribs showing, no muscle on him to speak of. I was fearful he wouldn't make it. We had named him Lazarus.

So, I put our neighbor's horse back on his property and proceeded back up to the barn to feed our animals. All the horses were present. Except Lazarus. With a sinking feeling in my stomach, I set off on a ride around our property looking for him. I couldn't find him anywhere, and I was fearful he had gone off and laid down somewhere to die. I rode the entire property not seeing him anywhere, and finished back at the gate to the rear lease pasture where the neighbor's buckskin was patiently staring at me. The star and snip markings on his forehead and nose matched our horse exactly.

Now, I've had a lot on my mind the past six weeks, and even though I had been feeding the horses, I had not been paying very close attention to them. They had plenty of green grass, fresh water, and as long as they were standing and eating, I was pretty happy to call them good. I called Shelley up at the house on my cell just to confirm I wasn't crazy.

Then I walked up to the gate and said one word, "Laz."

He flicked his ears at me and bobbed his head. This magnificent creature was our horse.

Now I'm not saying God performed a miracle on that horse. I'm also not saying He didn't. What I am saying is sometimes we need to be reminded that no matter how hard we try, how much control we want to have of a situation, or how badly we think we can affect the outcome, it's not up to us.

As Lazarus walked by me, I quietly murmured "Rise up, Lazarus," and chuckled to myself. Right on cue, Laz snorted, gave me a little side eye look, and took off on a beautiful gallop to join the rest of the horses.

Lesson learned. I'm NOT in control.

• • • •

WEEK 8 UPDATE - WE went to church for the first time since going to the hospital. It was great to be back among our friends and church family - an emotional and heartfelt welcome that left us both pretty tired. As we were about to leave, a church member approached and asked if Shelley remembered any type of out of body experience while in a coma.

Shelley still has a lot of short-term memory loss and doesn't remember much of anything after being taken to the hospital in an ambulance. She doesn't specifically remember any out of body experiences. One thing she does "remember" and has asked me about on several occasions is if she had two different brain injuries. She remembers being taken to the hospital, but then she thinks she remembers coming home for about a week before having another episode and going back to the hospital. That "week" coincides with the time she was in her coma, and when we talk about what she remembers specifically about that time, she just recalls being home and happy amongst her family and animals.

It reminds me of a song by Andy Griggs called "If Heaven." In the song he contemplates about what Heaven might be like:

"If Heaven was an hour, it would be twilight when the fireflies start their dancin' on the lawn. And supper's on the stove, and mammas laughin', And everybody's workin' day is done. If Heaven was a town it would be my town, on a summer day in 1985. And everything I wanted was out there waitin', and everyone I loved was still alive..."

I texted Shelley most days while she was in a coma so she would have something to read when she came out and have a sense of what had happened. Something about that song reminded me about one of the texts I sent:

"I feel optimistic today, like you are gathering yourself up to fight your way out. I had to leave the hospital for a couple of hours to take care of the animals, and everything was so beautiful at home, like it's just waiting for you to be here. Everything is green, the animals are fattening up, it was sunny and warm, and a butterfly was trying to land on Doogie's nose. I miss you and want you with me here now. I know it's selfish and I don't really care. I feel guilty being away from you, but things have to be kept in order for your return. I love you and will be back at your side in a little bit."

I did feel guilty sitting there watching the sun set in our little piece of Heaven. I had been so worried that Shelley's coma was like a dark prison, like a nightmare she couldn't escape. But that's not what she remembers.

Now, I'm not going to jump to any conclusions. There are quite a few accounts of out of body experiences or near-death occurrences that seem better suited answers for what that church member was hoping to hear. I really don't even want to speak for Shelley in this case. I just know it doesn't feel like it can get much closer to Heaven than sitting on our back porch at sunset, and that's where Shelley was waiting while her brain healed.

The Month of June

Weeks 9 & 10 Update: Since the beginning of my Billy Joel tribute, I have dedicated the song She's Got a Way to my wife. Lately it's had an even deeper impact since she is unable to perform with me or even attend my shows. This past Sunday, I was performing at Bernhardt Winery in front of a fairly large audience, and before playing that song, I briefly told the audience about Shelley's situation. I finished by telling them not to wait for tomorrow, and if they were attending with someone special tonight, to take a moment to get out on the dance area in front of the stage and hold their partner tight. I didn't expect nearly everyone to get up and dance together, it made it really tough to get through the song!

Later as I reflected on the moment, I recalled how many times I've procrastinated doing something, saying I'll do it tomorrow, or maybe I'll try it next time. Well, tomorrow is always tomorrow, and never today. If you knew there would not be an opportunity for tomorrow, what would you do differently today? I know, sounds cliché, until you actually live in the shadow of that very thing.

I remember as a child always saying, "See you in the morning" to my parents when going to bed. It was like I wanted them to know that was the plan, no matter what happened. Whether that was some form of childhood anxiety or not, I think we should maintain some of that "innocence" in our lives and not think it corny or silly to make sure loved ones know we love them before going to sleep, going to work, leaving for the store, or just about any situation.

I may have mentioned it before, Shelley's last words before slipping into her coma were "I love you," and the first time her eyes flickered open she mouthed the same words around her ventilator tube. Her priority was letting me know exactly how she felt.

Last night we went to the Ranger's game with her family. This was our biggest outing to date since being out of the hospital. We had a very enjoyable time, and I believe there were some mental barriers that we were able to break: a long trip in the car, a long walk in from the parking lot, being around a crowd and noise, and being out later than we are currently used to.

When the game was over and we were preparing to leave, I asked Shelley if we could take a picture together. We have tons of photos together from performing and politics. I know she also feels more self-conscious since being in the hospital, and taking pictures was already something she didn't care for a bunch. But I asked anyway. My reasoning was simple. She looked beautiful, and I wanted to be able to remember that night. Who knows if there will be another baseball game? Or even another picture? Why wait to dance tomorrow if you can dance tonight? Why wait to tell someone you love them when you can do it now?

People ask how we are doing, and I usually answer one day at a time. One beautiful day at a time.

• • • •

WEEK 11 UPDATE - SHELLEY was able to come to one of my shows with our family. It's a big undertaking; being away from home that long, a long drive, being around a lot of people and noise; but she did great! Overcoming those hurdles and the anxiety of not knowing if she can do it is a big step forward. I can't speak to it from experience, but from what Shelley shares with me, as a stroke survivor, there is a lack of surety when it comes to simple things that she used to do. Can I walk up that hill? Can I sit on the ground? Is the noise going to be too loud? Will I be able to talk to a lot of people? Passing these "tests" helps to reassure her of her recovery and rehabilitation.

We are finding ourselves in a very uncommon spot. I say we, because we are in this together, and there are unique challenges for both the patient and caregiver. So what is uncommon is that with the type of incident that occurred, most people don't make it to the hospital, of those that do, most don't survive surgery, and of those that do, most don't recover very well. Shelley has a device implanted in her brain that is so new, most doctors know very little about it. Her recovery has exceeded every doctor's expectation, and so they rarely have much to say at follow-up appointments. So, we feel like we don't have many answers, or many expectations for that matter. A lack of a definitive prognosis can induce a lot of fear and anxiety.

As the patient, it's hard for Shelley to accept that. As a caregiver, it's hard for me to help her navigate through those fears and concerns. When someone says to her, "I can't wait to hear you sing again," it is hard to find an appropriate response because we don't know if she will sing again. We really don't know anything at this point. Looking back over my posts I sometimes smack myself in disbelief at some of the cliché sounding rhetoric; but seriously, it's day by day, sometimes even hour by hour. We wake up with no expectations, and honestly, we are grateful just to wake up together one more time. Let's start there! Then the process of feeling out how she is feeling that day, medicating into a workable state, then moving forward from there is a bit of an adventure. So far, Shelley has risen to every occasion. That's the fighter in her not willing to concede anything moving backwards.

But even the strongest warriors have self-doubt at times, or sometimes they even get nicked in battle, so that's where I need to try and be the most supportive. My advice for anyone on the caregiver side of things, your top priority must be patience. Everything else falls into a good spot if I start with a large dose of patience. Empathy, motivation, anything else you can think of are all important ingredients too, but patience is the key.

It was great having Shelley in the audience last night. I probably tried to show off a little more than usual! But hey, who can blame me? She is always the most beautiful woman in the room, and it's nice to feel her eyes on me! When she reads this, she will probably roll her eyes, but for the first time in a long time my wife was in the audience, and that is a big victory!

• • • •

JUNE 29th at The Branch Church - Playing some keys tonight. Have not been here since Shelley's brain injury. I feel like I have a lot of people here to thank. This church is full of prayer warriors. It's humbling. No coincidence Gratitude is in the worship set tonight...

After the month of June, my updates curtailed themselves. Every day was pretty much the same. Medication, therapy, food, and watching baseball games, primarily the Texas Rangers, on TV. I was doing my best to refill my schedule and get back to work as well as taking care of the farm and the house. Shelley was in a cocoon of sorts. There was safety in her schedule, limited time in public, her favorite reclining chair, and animals. I knew there was a lot going on in her head. There were certain things frustrating her like some neuropathy in her right arm. Her sense of taste and smell were off and affected her appetite. I noticed she occasionally dragged her right foot when walking. Her speech was improving slowly, but it frustrated and embarrassed her when she slipped up on a word or lost her train of thought.

Personally, I was struggling with what God was wanting us to do with the experience we had been through and were still experiencing. There were a lot of people encouraging me to write a book, but it did not all make sense to me. In fact, it reminded me of how Shelley used to respond when people would ask her to do interviews about the salon incident in 2020. She would usually say, "What is there to talk about? I opened, I went to jail, I got out!"

Besides receiving a lot of testimony from people who had survived and recovered from aneurysms and strokes, I was also being engaged a lot by people who had relatives, spouses, and family members who did not make it. They had not experienced a miracle, and wanted to know why. They had prayed hard; their friends and church families had prayed. They had the best doctors. I did not have an answer for them. In fact, I could empathize with them. We had prayed constantly for my mom, and cancer had taken her in the most brutal of ways. This left me wondering what the testimony was supposed to be.

As He usually does, God communicated with me when He was ready to do so, and knew I was ready to receive it.

"I have a confession to make," Shelley said one day.

We proceeded to have a long and in-depth conversation about something that would change my perspective on everything. On April 2nd, two days before the aneurysm burst, Shelley and I were leading worship together at our church. During the song "Too Good to Not Believe," by Brandon Lake there is a section that contains some of the following lyrics:

We've seen cancer disappear.
We've seen broken bodies healed.
We've seen real life resurrection.
We've seen mental health restored.
Don't you tell me He can't do it.

While we were singing that song, Shelley stepped back from the front of the worship platform and put her microphone by her side for a while. I noticed, but assumed she either was feeling emotional about the song, or maybe had something in her throat and needed to cough. That wasn't it at all.

Shelley has suffered from migraine level headaches for twenty-five years. She has been to many different doctors, tried different types of medication, and even had a neck surgery to try and alleviate the problem, all to no avail. When these headaches hit, they put her in bed with the sheet over her head for the rest of the day, and she needed to take over-the-counter pain medication almost daily to keep them away the best she could.

Something in that song on April 2nd made her decide to give the problem to God. She pulled her microphone down from her mouth, stepped back, and prayed to God, asking Him to take the pain away.

Two days later she suffered the worst possible aneurysm and brain hemorrhage a person could have.

She told me all this as I listened carefully. When she was done, I remained silent, not only because I was unsure of what to say, but because she looked like she had something else to convey to me.

"I haven't had a headache like that since I woke up in the hospital," she said very deliberately.

The seriousness of this sank in relatively quickly.

"So, you are telling me, you prayed for God to take away your headaches, and one cerebral hemorrhage and seven strokes later, they are gone?"

Contemplation

Shelley's confession was at first shocking, but over time began to make more and more sense to me. One of the difficulties I was having before she revealed her prayer to me was how to respond to people who told me about similar situations they had experienced in their life, and how their prayers had not been heard. I could truly empathize with them, all the prayers in the world had not saved my mom.

At first, I did not have an answer for them. My wife by all accounts was supposed to be dead; however, there needed to be something deeper that God wanted me to not only learn, but witness to. I took it upon myself to process these things and do a little digging. I came up with the following conclusions.

First, we must decide if there is a divine plan for us.

Jeremiah 29:11 says, "'For I know the plans I have for you,'" declares the LORD, "'plans to prosper you and not to harm you, plans to give you hope and a future.'"

Some people believe that God has a plan for everyone, and the answer to prayers, or some cases not answering prayers is part of that divine plan. God, having infinite wisdom, may have reasons beyond human comprehension for answering or not answering specific prayers. Faith, trust, and hope are crucial components to knowing and understanding this.

Then, we need to consider free will.

Galatians 5:13 says, "You, my brothers and sisters, were called to be free. But do not use your freedom to indulge the flesh ; rather, serve one another humbly in love."

Additionally, Proverbs 16:9 says, "In their hearts humans plan their course, but the LORD establishes their steps."

God gave us free will, including the ability to choose repentance, as well as the ability to decide if we want to pray and what we want to pray for. More on that in a second!

We should also be aware that an unanswered prayer may be a time of spiritual growth and testing.

1 Peter 1:6-7 says, "In all this you greatly rejoice, though now for a little while you may have had to suffer grief in all kinds of trials. These have come so that the proven genuineness of your faith—of greater worth than gold, which perishes even though refined by fire—may result in praise, glory, and honor when Jesus Christ is revealed."

Being refined through trials often means God's answer to prayers may be delayed or unanswered for us to undergo the growth we are needing.

To better understand this miracle, we first need to understand what Shelley prayed for. She asked God to take away the physical pain she was experiencing in her head. She had lived with it for a long time, she had tried every available option to fix the problem, and had finally given it over to God. Since the hemorrhage, Shelley and I have discussed numerous times and agree that God's power is real, and not only should we respect it, but we should have a healthy fear of it. Choosing what we want to pray for, and how we pray for it just became a lot more serious for us when you put it into this context. Asking God to cure a headache resulted in a near death experience that took six months of Shelley's life away from her, and completely altered the trajectory of our lives. Remember when I said, you might want to be careful what you pray for?

We need to be thoughtful and deliberate when it comes to our prayers. This was evident not only in the result of Shelley's original prayer, but how things began to improve when the prayers for her recovery became more focused and intentional. It is also possible the outcomes of our prayers may not always be in line with our expectations, and the consequences of those outcomes may bring unexpected challenges.

When we pray or express our deepest desires, we often do so with a specific result in mind. It might be success, love, or healing. God's answer may unfold in a way we are not anticipating. We need to be careful about what we pray for, remember to approach life with humility, recognizing we don't have the foresight to see God's plan, and keep our hearts open to the lessons that come with the fulfillment, or sometimes, the denial of our heartfelt prayers. Taking all this into account, I felt I was better equipped to talk with someone who wanted to know why their prayers were not answered.

Even knowing what we felt we had learned; we still were not sure of what God's intention was for us. This is the point where I stopped writing this book. I was stuck and didn't know how to finish or how the testimony was supposed to conclude. That is when Shelley decided to spring one last surprise on me.

Summer did not go as well as we both hoped it would. Shelley went back to the hospital several times. The doctors assured us each time there were not any medical issues or complications with her surgeries, it was all balancing out all the medication she was taking. Those episodes were scary for all of us, though, and a reminder of where we had been just a few months before. As the summer wore on, with the doctor's approval, she began to slowly wean herself off the medication. All the therapy was also frustrating for her because the progress seemed so slow.

I was surprised by the number of people who said things to me like, "Good for you, sticking through this ordeal with her. A lot of people would have given up and left."

Seriously? How does a person even arrive at that decision as being reasonable?

Our first follow-up with Dr. Bhuva, the neurosurgeon who installed the flex embolization device, was particularly frightening for us. Shelley wanted some reassurances about the longevity of the device and statistics of people who had similar surgeries. The answer to Shelley's questions were non-existent. As it turns out, people requiring the device inserted into Shelley's brain usually don't survive, and those that do are usually left deficient mentally and physically. We were flabbergasted when the doctor told Shelley it was the first time she had ever talked to someone with the device operating properly in their head and there not be some underlying issues.

The more we learned, the less we wanted to know. Survival statistics, which were very few, were not promising. But Dr. Bhuva assured Shelley she should go out and live life. They would be monitoring her brain through CT scans and angiograms frequently, and if something looked like it was failing, they would go in and fix it. I think it really bothered Shelley, not because she feared death, but because she didn't want to let her family down. I kept trying to reassure her, give me your best every day, and don't worry about tomorrow. Five days, five weeks, five years, or five decades; I would take whatever I could get. God kept highlighting that thought for me, and I did my best to adopt that attitude myself; trying to give my best every day, one day at a time.

Shelley's brain scans still showed a lot of stroke damage, and doctors were not able to explain why she was walking, talking, and functioning like nothing had ever happened.

Even Shelley's last visit with the neurologist who had been responsible for the EVD insertion and removal was concerning. His comment when he walked in was, "Well you sure look better than your CT scan would indicate."

But life improved a little every day throughout the late summer and fall. We watched the Texas Rangers win a World Series. The neuropathy in her arm and leg disappeared. With the help of several doctors, she eliminated all but the crucial medicine from her regimen. We had some follow up appointments with several other neurologists and surgeons that confirmed for Shelley that she was ready to get back to living life. Finally, she had her six month follow up angiogram with Dr. Bhuva, and the results were better than we could have expected. Everything was healed and gone. There was no aneurysm, the blood was gone, the blood vessels looked normal, and everything was working the way it was supposed to. Amazingly, even the area of the brain damaged by the stroke was completely healed, and the doctor showed us a large blood vessel that had worked its way over from the other side of the brain and taken over the delivery of blood. The healing was complete.

My wife was back!

I did not expect her to jump right back into life where we were on April 4th before the incident. But I was hoping we could finally start to return to something that would be a little more normal for us. That is when I got the phone call.

"I'm going to run for office again."

I don't remember exactly what I said, but I know for sure I didn't try to give my best that day. In fact, I didn't talk much to Shelley for a couple days. I was so angry. I finally explained to her that after giving everything I had to save her life, after living through hell for what seemed like eternity, having to help her struggle through therapy and rehabilitation, I finally felt like I was getting my wife back, only to have her decide to do something that was an immense strain on our family, her health, and our relationship. We had survived the senate campaign in 2020, and after running for state house of representatives just two years prior, she had decided enough was enough and had me throw away all the political material we had accumulated. We both had been happy to move on out of that season of our lives. This desire to run for office again was not just surprising, it was shocking.

We talked about it a lot for a couple days, but it was God that had the last word for me. I woke up one morning and clearly knew if I had been able to get through the past six months successfully with His help, I could certainly navigate my way through one more political campaign. Additionally, if this was the catalyst that got my wife to become active again and start living her life, I had to honor that feeling she was having.

Something else spiritual was also moving and it was permeating my shows. I had initially just taken a few minutes at each show to update people on how Shelley was doing, but now it had become a short testimony. I talked about what had happened to us, but also encouraged people to quit putting off something simple like dancing with their spouse. I asked people to get up and dance together while I played a song dedicated to Shelley, reminding them we never really know if there will be a tomorrow. Not only was the dance floor packed with people dancing, I had numerous people approach me after shows thanking me for reminding them how precious our time with one another really is. I also had the opportunity to pray with people who were experiencing hardship or loss. I heard great testimonies from others, and began to see what all this journey was meant for.

The same was happening for Shelley as she began campaigning. People had been exposed to her "human side," and she was no longer this folk hero people had seen on television. Everywhere she went, she told people the amazing testimony of how her life was saved and changed by God.

As if there were not enough miracles in this story, one more popped up while Shelley was campaigning. One evening at a meet and greet, a young man walked in. He introduced himself to Shelley and she quickly remembered him as one of the first responders that had been in the ambulance that came to our house in April. As they discussed what happened, he told her something that still sends shivers down my spine. He had been initially unable to get a needle successfully into the vein in her arm. That night, his regular partner was out sick, and he had a substitute riding along with him that rarely if ever worked with that team. It just so happened this EMT was extremely skilled, and in his words, was as good or better than any doctor. He jumped in, got the IV started, and made sure Shelley started getting the medication she needed for the long trip to the hospital. Without him being present, Shelley might not have ever made it to the first emergency room.

I have watched countless people come up to Shelley while she is out campaigning and just put their hand on her arm, look at her, and start crying. It is humbling to see how many people have been impacted by what happened to us.

So, how does it all end?

That is the beautiful part of this story, we don't know.

God answered Shelley's prayer, to take away her headaches. The trial and refinement process nearly killed her. It put immense strain on all of us, but not only did she end up stronger and healthier than she was before the incident, she had the opportunity to feel God's grace and experience faith.

Speaking with someone who is very well studied theologically, our conversation at one point turned into an interesting question. Do angels envy humans?

His point was they surely must, because there is one thing they don't have that we have as humans. We can experience faith. Think about it for a minute. Angels know for a fact that God exists. He is something they see and experience very tangibly. As humans, we only know God through faith. We get to experience God and His love for us through very different eyes than the angels. What Shelley and I got to experience heaped immeasurable amounts of faith and hope into our spiritual lives. The only reasonable explanation for what happened to us was the work of God.

I couldn't explain it well to anyone, no matter how hard I tried. I even tried to describe the feeling I was having when having lunch with pastor Jason one day. I could only describe that the first time we were able to return to church I looked at everyone a little differently. They were staring at Shelley like she was a ghost, and I imagine that I would have too, knowing how close she had been to death. But for me, the best way I could describe it was that I felt a lot older and a little wiser, even though we had only been gone a few months. It felt like walking into your childhood home forty years later. Something was very different about me, and I couldn't put my finger on it.

But as I wrapped up this book, it started coming into focus. I am beginning to understand what God wanted of us. He pulled the curtain back just a little bit. He let His light shine brightly on us for just a moment. He answered prayers swiftly. He performed a miracle, and then He told us to spread the word. The impression Shelley and I were both given was, "Tell them what I did for you."

Since that first post I made on the night of April 4th, millions of people have engaged with us in seeing a beautiful miracle take place, and after roughly fifty-seven thousand words, I know what the feeling is. I know what I am supposed to say. I know what the message is supposed to be.

God exists.

Not only does God exist, He wants us to know Him, not just by seeing and hearing Him like the angels, but through the mystery of faith and hope.

And sometimes by assuring us through a blessed miracle.

    • • • •

BLESSED ASSURANCE, Jesus is mine!
  Oh, what a foretaste of glory divine!
  Heir of salvation, purchase of God,
  Born of His Spirit, washed in His blood.
  This is my story, this is my song,
  Praising my Savior all the day long;
  This is my story, this is my song,
  Praising my Savior all the day long.

    • • • •

PERFECT SUBMISSION, perfect delight,
  Visions of rapture now burst on my sight;
  Angels, descending, bring from above
  Echoes of mercy, whispers of love.

    • • • •

THIS IS MY STORY, THIS is my song,
  Praising my Savior all the day long;
  This is my story, this is my song,
  Praising my Savior all the day long.

    • • • •

PERFECT SUBMISSION, all is at rest,

I in my Savior am happy and blest,
Watching and waiting, looking above,
Filled with His goodness, lost in His love.

• • • •

THIS IS MY STORY, THIS is my song,
Praising my Savior all the day long;
This is my story, this is my song,
Praising my Savior all the day long.

• • • •

GOD EXISTS. HIS MIRACLES surround us. All we need to do is watch and listen. Thank you to everybody who prayed for us. Thank you to everyone who supported us. Thank you to our family, our friends, our church families, and to all our new brothers and sisters in Christ. And thank you to God, for showing us the way and touching our lives in such a powerful and magnificent way.

• • • •

THIS IS OUR STORY. This is our song. This is our blessed assurance and our message to you.